Getting to Know You!

Social Skills Curriculum
for Grades 6 - 9

by
Dennis Hanken, Ed.S.
and
Judith Kennedy, Ed.S.

ISBN No. 1-930572-01-8

Library of Congress Catalog No. 00-100780

Publisher—

Educational Media Corporation®
Box 21311
Minneapolis, MN 55421-0311

(612) 781-0088

Production Editor—

Don L. Sorenson

Graphic Designer—

Earl R. Sorenson

Dedication

This book is dedicated to our grandchildren:

Judith: **Zachary David King** 10/20/94

Dennis: **Jordyn Christie Sacrison** 12/16/99

The future of our world is in the hands of the next generation. May they benefit from our experiences, but be open enough to carry the torch of knowledge on to greater heights.

About the Authors

Dennis Hanken and his wife, Wendy, are the parents of three daughters. He has polished his own social skills and developed an awareness of the need for social skills training in his 28 years working with youth in an educational setting. His fellow workers and students enjoy his keen sense of humor, empathy, and enjoyment of life. He is currently a school psychologist in the Rapid City School System in South Dakota.

Judith Kennedy is married and the parent of two children, two stepchildren, a daughter-in-law, and a grandson. A focus of her life has always been to assist children to interact respectfully, live their lives fully, and achieve their potential. She has thirty years experience working with youth and is currently a school psychologist.

Acknowledgments

We thank "Dear Wally" publishers, Guideposts Book Division, 16 East 34th St., New York, NY 10016, for the use of the "Dear Wally" letters to support our curriculum and *Aesop's Fable* which complement our lessons. Thanks also to Laura Harrison for her great perspective of middle school children.

Table of Contents

Relieving Stress

Making Decisions

Handling Agression

Self-Acceptance

Foreword

This is the third volume of *Getting to Know You: Social Skills Curriculum.*

The first two volumes present the curriculum for grades one through three and grades four and five. Those two volumes were very well received, so we decided to write a curriculum for grades six through nine. Our first two volumes have been recognized nationally as Exemplary Mental Health Programs because of their success in preventing violence. Like the first two volumes, this volume is based on best practices in psychology.

We continue with the same format for the lessons: Stating the objective, identifying the materials needed, establishing the need, outlining the procedures, comments, and identifying extended activities. In the procedures section, three steps are followed: Model the skill, role play with feedback, and transfer training. Research indicates these are the areas to be included in a successful social skills curriculum.

So, what is new with this volume? First of all, we have added some new skills in each area. Since we are writing for adolescents, the developmental level in the "Establish the Need" section has been adapted to this age group. We used several formats to show the reason for acquiring the skill. Students at this age often love to act and be on stage. The role play portion of each lesson capitalizes on this while engaging students to become more involved. We added a new feature called "Gender Differences" because some of these skills are experienced differently with one gender or the other.

Our curriculum is based on the premise that misbehavior can be the result of the student not knowing what is expected. Therefore, the curriculum teaches students the skills to be successful in school and in interpersonal relationships. Beginning to teach the prosocial approach to social skills acquisition in kindergarten is optimal, because it builds a foundation for a common philosophy or vision for the success of students. Teachers can save many hours of relentless reteaching when all the staff participates in a common social skills curriculum school wide.

Our philosophy with adolescents is that they have an enormous amount of energy, inquisitiveness, and social awareness. They tend to react spontaneously. Adolescents need guidance and assistance when experiencing turbulence in their quest for answers to their life's problems. This curriculum gives the school a way to deal with *all* students, and to accommodate the unique developmental needs of adolescents.

Some of the areas we cover in this curriculum are:
1. Family Structure
2. Peer Relationships
3. Adolescents in School
4. Moral and Value Development
5. Physical Development
6. Sexual Development
7. Cognitive Development

We hope you find this volume as useful as our first two.

Introduction

Why teach social skills? The question of whether it is the responsibility of schools to teach socially appropriate behavior has been debated for years, but the fact remains that educators are dealing increasingly with maladjusted behavior. According to statistics from the U. S. Department of Education, three to six percent of the school population have significant social adjustment problems. Many students who enter kindergarten come from homes that are dysfunctional, abusive, economically impoverished, or that contain alcohol or drug addicted parents.

More children than ever come from nontraditional families with parents who are underemployed and even in their teens. Professionals report that the decline of the family unit, changing morals, the step-family, drug and alcohol abuse, working parents, television, and rising crime rate are just a few of the things that have caused children to be less proficient in appropriate social behavior. However, even children who benefit from exposure to appropriate social behavior at home, church, or in their communities have a need to learn the parameters of expected behaviors in school.

Teaching social skills helps eliminate problematic behaviors. Educators are then free to teach academics rather than deal with disruptive behaviors. A good social skills curriculum teaches the appropriate behavior rather than correcting the inappropriate behavior. This approach has proven in field studies to decrease inappropriate behavior while increasing the desired behavior.

In the last ten years, social skills research and curriculums have appeared all over the United States. Journal articles have focused on this area. Social skills training programs have become an integral component of special education curricula (Schumaker, Pederson, Hazel, and Meyer, 1983). However, experience has shown that teaching social skills in isolation fails to transfer those skills back to the regular classroom, playground, community, and home (Gresham, 1986). An additional disadvantage to teaching social skills only to children in special education is that it fails to reach other at-risk youth who do not qualify for special education programs.

Who benefits from learning social skills?

- Children who are either withdrawn or aggressive;
- Children who are developing normally, but who have periodic deficits in prosocial skill behaviors;
- Children who have learning disabilities, communication disorders, behavioral problems, or other handicaps (Burstien, 1986). These children tend to interact more with teachers than with peers.

Effective social skills curricula. The authors of this curriculum have researched many books, curricula, and theories on social skills training to identify the ingredients of an effective social curriculum.

These ingredients are:

1. Use a proactive approach—teach all students the desired behaviors rather than spend time correcting disruptive behaviors.
2. Teach the curriculum daily just as one does math and reading.
3. Involve all personnel in the school in the curriculum so the desired behavior is reinforced in all environments.
4. Use a common language that all personnel and children identify as steps to the desired behavior.
5. Model and role play each skill component.
6. Involve parents in reinforcing the skills.

The *Getting to Know You* Curriculum. This curriculum is well researched and has each of these ingredients. It has been field tested in schools where it helped decrease maladaptive behaviors by 70% This curriculum can do the same for you. It is designed to be used in the regular classroom where it will benefit all students regardless of race, creed, color, or academic ability. It was developed in a city school system in a rural region with a diverse student population to include a large percentage of Lakota Native Americans and U.S. Air Force families.

The authors believe that social skills can be taught like academics in a positive mode rather than using punishment as a means to control social behavior. This is called a prosocial skills approach and focuses on teaching new skills rather than correcting maladaptive behavior.

Our philosophy is: students come to school with varying levels of social skill development. Research shows that new social skills are best learned by using the components of modeling, role playing, performance feedback, and transfer training. Providing a student with correct strategies and practice to increase performance works for both academics and social skills.

Our component model for the development of social skills is:

Model the skill—the teacher demonstrates "Think Aloud" steps.

Role play with feed back—the students rehearse and practice skill steps with positive feedback and corrections.

Transfer activities—the children will use these newly learned skills in real-life situations.

Our instruction model includes:

Identifying the skill/establishing the need

Identifying situations in which the skill is needed

Presenting the steps of the skill

Modeling the skill (teacher or older students)

"Think Aloud"—internal dialogue or practice in your mind of the skill steps

Guided role playing—practice for students using appropriate role playing of new skill (some authors recommend an additional inappropriate example for teaching purposes)

Dennis Hanken, Ed.S. and Judith Kennedy, Ed.S.

Positive feedback—corrections

Transfer training to generalize the skill

Maintenance activities

Prosocial skills to be covered in the manual:

I. Classroom Skills

II. Friendship Skills

III. Expressing Feelings

IV. Relieving Stress

V. Making Decisions

VI. Handling Aggression

VII. Self Acceptance

This curriculum has lesson plans for each skill that are easy to implement for the regular classroom teacher. Each lesson contains an objective which states the purpose of the lesson, lists the materials needed, and cites a reason for acquiring the skill. The teacher then models the skill, after which the students practice an appropriate example of the skill. An inappropriate example of the skill is included in "Helpful Hints" to contrast the right and wrong way the skill is done. This format is based on current research which outlines that children learn best when given a model of a behavior and time to practice the skill with feedback.

An important component of this model is transfer training. Many social skills programs fail because they do not provide the student with opportunities to apply the social skill they learned in real-life situations. This model provides homework assignments to be done in other areas of the school, at home or in the community and with peers. Assigning these activities and seeing that they are completed is an integral component of this model, and will make the difference in successful generalization of these skills to other environments.

The end of each lesson contains comments, if needed, and extended activities which can be used if the students have not fully mastered the skill. These are enjoyable activities the students will perform in real life situations to more fully reinforce the learning of these skills.

Some lessons may need to be taught several days so that all students learn the skill, while other lessons may require only one teaching. It will be beneficial to review the previously learned skills in order to ensure mastery.

When you decide as a group or school to use this curriculum, you many want to pick two to four skills to focus on each quarter of the year. Review these skills at the end of the school year. By the time your kindergarten children are in the upper grades, they should be good role models for the younger children in your school.

Our intent is for this curriculum to be easy as well as fun to teach. We hope you and your students enjoy it.

Instructions for Using this Curriculum

1. This curriculum is based on well-researched practices. One of the reasons for its documented success is the "Think Aloud" strategies. These strategies are actually the internal dialogue we recommend be taught to students. The consistent use of the "Think Aloud" strategies by all school staff provides the basis for the success of this curriculum in decreasing undesirable behavior, while increasing the desired social skills. You will have better success changing the behavior of your students if all personnel are trained to use the common language in the "Think Aloud" strategies. This includes principals, secretarial staff, lunchroom, and auxiliary staff.

2. The posters reinforce the "Think Aloud" strategies. They follow each lesson and should be enlarged and displayed in the classrooms, hallways, and other areas of your school. Copy the student awards at the end of each section and present them to your students to reinforce the skills learned.

3. Each lesson has a story, activity, or discussion to "Establish the Need." Additional stories or activities under "Extended Activities" also will reinforce the skill in the lesson.

4. There is a sample letter to the parents should you choose to elicit parental support prior to beginning this curriculum. (page 14)

5. This curriculum is based on the teaching methods of modeling the skill, providing opportunity for the students to role play, and reinforcing their skills with feedback. It is important that you actually model the desired skill using the "Think Aloud" strategies so your students can see the desired behavior.

6. The role play section of each lesson is meant to provide an opportunity for your students to practice the desired skill. This is the time to give feedback and correct any behavior. Research results are inconclusive as to whether role playing an incorrect example of each behavior is helpful for the students in learning the desired behavior. Some of the leaders in the field of social skill development believe that students learn the desired skill better if they are able to practice the contrast behavior; other feel this is unnecessary and a distraction. We have sometimes included a contrast role play under "Helpful Hints." You may use it at your discretion, knowing the needs of your students.

7. The most common reason for the failure of a social skills curriculum is in the lack of those skills generalizing to other environments. We correct this by providing "Transfer Training" activities to be done in other environments.

8. We hope you enjoy this curriculum, have fun with it, and use your own creativity to expand the lessons. We believe that for it to be the most effective, the skills should be taught in the order presented.

9. Gender Differences—This may help explain the differences between how boys and girls react differently to various skills and situations.

Suggestions for Teaching Social Skills

Now that you have the "why" and the ingredients, how do you start? Many schools start social skills curriculums, but they only last one to two years because staff lose interest, have other priorities, and don't see immediate impact.

Therefore, your school needs to know that a 4 to 5 year plan is essential. Start out slowly with classroom skills or friendship skills. Then proceed to other skills that are more difficult to master. Remember, all the staff, certified and non-certified, have to agree to do this. Set up meetings to define the needs of the school. Help each other to refine the program. Some skills will take longer to master than others. Listening, for example, is a life long skill that needs to be reinforced every year.

Each year you can set several skills as your targets and also review skills from previous years. Take a skill such as "Interrupting." Let's say you are going to teach the skill on Monday. Proceed through the whole lesson. Then, the rest of the week, review "Think Aloud" strategies. Do this review for two weeks and then as needed throughout the year. If problems arise, gently remind your students to repeat—either individually or in a group—the "think aloud" strategies. This skill will probably need to be reviewed. Plus, new students to the school are not aware of previous skills taught. Keep the "Think Aloud" strategy posters on the walls every year to remind your students of common language.

Another suggestion is to have the principal reinforce whatever skill you are working on when he or she does announcements. Leadership helps keep the skills moving and reinforces the positive aspects and results. You can also involve parents through parent/teacher conferences, PTA meetings, and newsletters. Community involvement is essential. Most parents want their children to have good social skills, but parents need help reinforcing them at home.

Some staff or schools are always changing curriculum—looking for the magic answer to solve all problems. Let's be realistic. Changing behavior and starting new programs *involves* hard work, determination, enthusiasm, and a concentrated effort over a long period of time. Schools with positive philosophies and a staff who work as a team to change negative behaviors always succeed because children and parents know what the expectations are.

There is no set way or philosophy to teaching social skills. Schools that stay with a social skills programs and: (1) are consistent and positive, (2) follow through with lessons, (3) involve parents; (4) define and refine programs through committee and staff meetings, (5) have all staff involved, (6) use common language, and (7) establish long term goals (4 to 5 years) will survive. The results will be positive benefits to the children. Both parents and teachers will be working together to improve the social skills of all children so they can learn in a positive environment.

Our Class is Studying Social Skills!

Dear Parent::

Our class is beginning a social skills curriculum. Your child will be learning better ways to resolve conflict, make friends and follow rules. These skills will help your children feel better about themselves, make decisions, handle stress and choose the best action in a given situation. Our belief is that in teaching children appropriate social skills, there is less need for correction of behavior.

We ask that you help reinforce these social skills at home. For each lesson there will be an activity to do at home. The purpose of these activities is to help your children do these skills in any environment.

There are seven areas of skills your children will learn with specific lessons under each area. The seven areas are:

1. Classroom Skills
2. Friendship Skills
3. Expressing Feelings
4. Relieving Stress
5. Solving Problems
6. Replacement Skills
7. Self Acceptance

Thank you for your support. Please call me if you have any concerns or questions.

Your Children's Teacher

Teacher's Screening Checklist

_____   _____   _____

Student's Name   Rated By   Date

Directions:

Circle the appropriate letter for each question. Rate this child in comparison with other children in the class.

Key:

5—Very often—means daily occurrence

3—Sometimes—means 2 to 3 times a week

1—Seldom—means 0 occurrence

I. Classroom Skills

1. Does the student listen to instructions or directions?	5	4	3	2	1
2. Does the student complete assignments on time?	5	4	3	2	1
3. Does the student follow classroom rules?	5	4	3	2	1
4. Does the student cooperate with a work partner?	5	4	3	2	1
5. Is the student prepared for class?	5	4	3	2	1

II. Interpersonal Relationships

1. Is the student accepted by most of his or her classmates?	5	4	3	2	1
2. Does the student have one or more friends?	5	4	3	2	1
3. Is the student often a victim of teasing?	5	4	3	2	1
4. Is the student respectful of other's property?	5	4	3	2	1
5. Is the student excluded by his or her peers?	5	4	3	2	1

III. Identifying and Expressing Feelings

1. Can the student express feelings in an appropriate way?	5	4	3	2	1
2. Does the student show understanding of other's feelings?	5	4	3	2	1
3. Does the student express unusual or extreme feelings?	5	4	3	2	1

IV. Relieving Stress

1. Can the student accept losing or failing?	5	4	3	2	1
2. Does the student handle changes in the daily routine?	5	4	3	2	1
3. Does the student over or under react to situations?	5	4	3	2	1
4. Does the student show signs of anxiety, nervousness, or stress?	5	4	3	2	1
5. Does the student defend his or her rights?	5	4	3	2	1

V. Problem Solving/Decision Making

1. Does the student accept responsibility for his or her actions?	5	4	3	2	1
2. Is the student able to make a decision independently?	5	4	3	2	1
3. Does the student overreact to minor problems?	5	4	3	2	1

VI. Replacement Skills

1. Does the student express anger appropriately?	5	4	3	2	1
2. Does the student avoid fights?	5	4	3	2	1
3. Does the student work out problems with friends by talking and compromising?	5	4	3	2	1
4. Does the student avoid situations which may cause problems?	5	4	3	2	1

VII. Self Acceptance

1. Does the student like himself or herself?	5	4	3	2	1
2. Does the student avoid putting down self and others?	5	4	3	2	1
3. Does the student tolerate differences in others?	5	4	3	2	1

Lesson 1:   Being Prepared for Class

Objective: Students will have material needed to participate in a specific class.

Materials Needed: None.

Establish the Need: Read this story about "Beth's Dilemma" and discuss it with your class.

Beth stopped at her locker to put away her science book. Amy was getting books from her nearby locker. Amy said, "Say, Beth, are you going to the soccer game tonight?" Beth replied, "No, I have dance class at 7:00, and I have to baby-sit my niece after school." Just then the bell rang. Beth's next class was algebra, and she hadn't found her book or her homework because she had used the passing time to talk.

1. What do you think will happen now?
2. What might Beth have done to be ready for class?

Procedures:

Step 1:   Model the skill:

Model using "Think Aloud" strategies—being ready for math class.

1. What materials do I need?
2. Do I need a book, pencil, or paper?
3. Do I have homework?
4. Check to see if I have everything I need.

Step 2:   Role play with feedback:

A. Role play being prepared for language arts class.

B. Elicit from your students ways to ensure being organized and prepared for class.

1. Folder/notebook for each subject.
2. Folder or pocket for homework.
3. Special materials (calculators, slide rulers) stored with the notebook for that subject area.
4. Organizational tips for lockers.

Step 3:   Transfer training

A. **School:** Ask another teacher to give feedback to your students on being prepared for that class.

B. **Home/Community:** Ask the parents to discuss with their students and decide how to make sure that all materials are ready to return to school each day.

C. **Peers:** Have your students list the things they will need for a sports activity, i.e., soccer.

Comments: Students with Attention Deficit Hyperactivity Disorder (ADHD) may have particular difficulty with this.

Extended Activities:

1. Have your students list the things they need to take along on a weekend at the lake.
2. Have them share their system for being organized.
3. Have each student develop a system to organize materials for school to be checked by teacher.

Lesson 1:   Being Prepared for Class

1. What materials do I need?

2. Do I need a book, pencil, or paper?

3. Do I have homework?

4. Check to see if I have everything I need.

CLASSROOM SKILLS

Lesson 2: Ways to be Organized

Objective: Students will develop an organizational system for their school materials.

Materials Needed: Have your students bring binders, folders, or whatever you have discussed to develop an organizational system. Have your own system to demonstrate.

Establish the Need: Read this story about "Disorganization Causes Problems" and discuss it with your class.

Zachary rushed down the hall to English, sliding in the door just as the bell rang. As he walked to his desk, papers were falling out of his notebook. It was no wonder; papers were bulging out every direction from his three-ring notebook. The first thing Ms. Grammar did was to ask her students to tell her the plot of the story, *Julius Caesar,* which had been assigned as homework. Zachary opened his notebook and looked through every paper, but he couldn't find his homework.

1. What are some things Zachary could do to be sure to find his homework?
2. What do you do with your homework to make sure you can find it?
3. Would different color folders/notebooks help in organizing the work for each class?

Procedures:

Step 1: Model the skill:

With your organizational system, model using "Think Aloud" strategies—how to find your homework page.

1. Open my folder.
2. Locate my materials.
3. Put the papers back where they belong.

Step 2: Role play with feedback:

A. Divide your students into groups of three; tell them to demonstrate their organizational systems to each other.
B. Have one student from each group demonstrate to the class the best of the group's ideas for organization.

Step 3: Transfer training

A. **School:** Ask another teacher to evaluate your students' organizational systems and practices.
B. **Home/Community:** As a class, draft a letter to parents stating the optimal components of an organizational system.
C. **Peers:** In small groups, have your students organize a party, including invitations, food, and entertainment.

Comments: Again, students with Attention Deficit Hyperactivity Disorder will have more trouble with this.

Extended Activities:

1. Have your students organize their closet or room at home and share with the class their system of organizing.
2. Have them outline or draw the components of an optimal organizational system for them.

Lesson 2:   Ways to be Organized

1. Open my folder.

2. Locate my materials.

3. Put the papers back where they belong.

CLASSROOM SKILLS

Lesson 3: Listening

Objective: Students will be able to restate what someone says to them.

Materials Needed: None.

Establish the Need: Read this story entitled "Are You Listening?" and discuss it with your class.

Stephanie and Melanie were sitting at a picnic table in the park. Stephanie seemed upset. Melanie said, "So, what's up, Steph?" Stephanie sighed and said, "Oh, you probably don't really want to know." "Of course I do," huffed Melanie. "Well , you know that new boy, David? Well, I asked him to the dance and he laughed and walked off. I was so embarrassed," said Stephanie. "Oh, well, if you want to hear about embarrassed.... Mr. Harvey called on me in science yesterday and... blah, blah, blah," replied Melanie.

1. How do you think Stephanie feels?
2. Was Melanie listening?
3. What might Stephanie have done so she felt Melanie heard her?

Procedures:

Step 1:　Model the skill:

Model using "Think Aloud" strategies—listening attentively.

(1) Look in the person's eyes. (2) Wait your turn to talk. (3) Think about what the person is saying. (4.) Rephrase what the speaker has said, "So, I hear you saying...."

Step 2:　Role play with feedback:

A. In pairs, have your students take turns talking for two minutes about which performers are their favorites. To ensure listening, have them report the other's favorite after this exercise and check for accuracy.

B. Do an auditory memory game. Have each student say one word—any word—going around the room and adding a new word each time after reciting all the previous ones. The point is to see how many words can be remembered. It is also fun to use words in categories, i.e., song titles, movies, foods.

Step 3:　Transfer training

A. **School:** Ask another teacher to model and reinforce "Listening Think Aloud" strategies.

B. **Home/Community:** Assign for homework reporting to the class one thing remembered from listening to the news.

C. **Peers:** Give an assignment to listen to one other person tonight.

Comments: Listening is hard, even for adults. Nelson (1998) described Deep Listening—a 3-step process: (1) Pause. (2) Repeat the message internally. (3) Search out feelings.

Extended Activities:

1. Ask students to relay examples of good and poor listeners in the media.
2. Discuss how many times each student needed to listen to the lyrics of a popular song to understand the words.
3. Silence is a component of listening. Discuss.

Lesson 3: Listening

1. Look in the person's eyes.

2. Wait your turn to talk.

3. Think about what the person is saying.

4. Rephrase what the speaker has said, "So, I hear you saying...."

CLASSROOM SKILLS

Dennis Hanken, Ed.S. and Judith Kennedy, Ed.S.

Lesson 4:   Study Habits

Objective: Students will demonstrate mastery of study skills.

Materials Needed: 3x5 file cards, a highlighter for each student.

Establish the Need: Read this story entitled "Studying" and discuss it with your class.

There was a unit test coming up in health class. Robby read the material over and over. It was boring, and he had a hard time keeping his attention on the subject. He felt he should be prepared because he had read it all. The next morning when Robby got his test, he saw it was a "fill in the blanks" type test. He hadn't studied to memorize details. He had read only to be familiar with the content. He couldn't remember the details needed to complete the sentences, so he did poorly on the test.

1. Name some ways Robby could have studied to be better prepared.
2. Tell some of the ways you study to prepare for tests.

Procedures:

Step 1:   Model the skill:

Model using "Think Aloud" strategies—ways to study.

1. Name what I need to learn.
2. What is the best way to study?
3. Gather your supplies and begin.

Step 2:   Role play with feedback:

A. In groups of three or four, have your students prepare study materials for an upcoming test.
B. Have them list the study habits that work best for them.

Step 3:   Transfer training

A. **School:** Have your students prepare materials for a test or project. Evaluate each student's material.
B. **Home/Community:** Have them design a study area in their own homes.
C. **Peers:** Have your students form study groups to study for the next test.

Comments: Give examples for studying that include environment, comfort, memorization, time of day, webbing, and outlining. Each person needs different elements.

Extended Activities:

1. Have your students explain numerous approaches to studying and evaluate which is most effective for them.
2. Teach note taking, graphing, outlining, and webbing as techniques.
3. Take your class to the library after teaching a unit on research. Have them research a topic for a class presentation.

Lesson 4:   Study Habits

1. Name what I need to learn.

2. What is the best way to study?

3. Gather your supplies and begin.

CLASSROOM SKILLS

Dennis Hanken, Ed.S. and Judith Kennedy, Ed.S.

Lesson 5: Following Oral Directions

Objective: Students will correctly carry out multistep directions.

Materials Needed: Have various board games (i.e., *Monopoly*, *Scrabble*) for Transfer Training C.

Establish the Need: Read this story and discuss it with your class.

Lost in Space

Jordan was piloting the spaceship back to earth. Amy, the copilot, was reading directions off the manual for the return to earth. They had been exploring outer space for four years and were anxious to get home. "Turn left at asteroid 9, fly under the Milky Way, a sharp left to avoid Soviet satellite 949, and bank right toward Cape Kennedy," read Amy. Flying well beyond the speed of light, Jordan had to react quickly to the directions to stay on track. He went left at asteroid 9 and under the Milky Way, but then he took a sharp right instead of left. "Oh, no," said Amy. "Now we are headed deep in space again."

1. Have you ever made a mistake by misunderstanding directions?

2. What can happen when we misunderstand directions?

Procedures:

Step 1:	Model the skill:

Model using "Think Aloud" strategies—following a 6-step oral direction.

1. Listen.

2. What do I do first, second, next?

3. Do it.

Step 2:	Role play with feedback:

Give a 6-step oral direction by row or group. Discuss.

Step 3:	Transfer training

A. **School:** Ask another teacher to give a 6-step direction and feedback to students.

B. **Home/Community:** Have your students give 6- or more-step direction to each other on how to get from their homes to school. The listening student draws a map from the directions.

C. **Peers:** Group your students and hand out games. One student gives oral directions to others.

Comments: Meeting new people presents problems for some people in remembering the names. Provide opportunities to practice this.

Extended Activities: Have your students write skits showing good and poor listening examples.

Give directions to a "treasure hunt." Have your students draw a map as you give directions.

Lesson 5: Following Oral Directions

1. Listen.

2. What do I do first, second, next?

3. Do it.

CLASSROOM SKILLS

Lesson 6:   Completing Assignments on Time

Objective: Students will complete and turn in assignments by a due date.

Materials Needed: Worksheets relevant to class, free time activities.

Establish the Need: Have two student volunteers read and act out the following skit.

Work, Work, Work

Molly: Hi, Jo, did you get your math assignment done?

Jo: Heck, no. It's not due until later today. I thought I'd get it done at lunch.

Molly: But you always sit and talk at lunch. How are you going to get your math done?

Jo: Well, maybe I'll skip science and do it then.

Molly: But you need to get your science class project done because it is due tomorrow.

Jo: Gosh, work, work, work. When is a kid supposed to have fun?

    1. What are some other choices Jo could have made for getting her math assignment done?

    2. Where has Jo set her priorities?

Procedures:

Step 1:   Model the skill:

Model using "Think Aloud" strategies—completing and turning in an assignment on time.

    1. What do I need to have done?

    2. When is it due?

    3. When is the best time to do it?

    4. Start working.

    5. Hand in your completed work.

Step 2:   Role play with feedback:

Give out the worksheets. Obtain from your students the time they will need to complete worksheet. Set a timer for that time. Any students done early may do a free-time activity.

Step 3:   Transfer training

    A. **School:** Give an assignment (i.e., book report) that is due in three days. Recognize those students who complete and hand it in on time.

    B. **Home/Community:** Have your students pick one thing they need to have done outside of school, when it needs to be done, and how they will complete it on time.

    C. **Peers:** Lead a discussion with your students on ideas for completing out of school work/responsibilities on time.

Comments: This is a crucial skill for success in life. Discuss non-producers. How does cooperative learning enter into this area?

Extended Activities: Assign an activity which needs to be done in groups by a certain date.

Lesson 6: Completing Assignments on Time

1. What do I need to have done?

2. When is it due?

3. When is the best time to do it?

4. Start working.

5. Hand in your completed work.

CLASSROOM SKILLS

Lesson 7: Ignoring Distractions

Objective: Students will ignore distractions and keep working.

Materials Needed: Radio.

Establish the Need: Explain to your students that it is hard for some people to work if there is movement, noise, or odors. Explain that because of the makeup of people's brains, it is harder for some to work if there are distractions. Elicit from your students the times they found it hard to concentrate. Give examples when you find it hard to concentrate.

Procedures:

Step 1:   Model the skill:

Model using "Think Aloud" strategies—ignoring distractions.

1. What is distracting me?
2. What do I need to do to keep working?
   A. Ignore
   B. Move
   C. Ask the other person to stop
3. Keep working.

Step 2:   Role play with feedback:

A. Ask your students to work for two minutes while you keep changing the station on a radio with volume turned to quite loud.

B. Ask for feedback. Was it or was it not distracting?

Step 3:   Transfer training

A. **School:** Ask another teacher to reinforce students who stay on task and ignore distractions.

B. **Home/Community:** Elicit a discussion from students on what conditions they need when they are doing homework. Does TV bother them? How about someone talking on the phone?

C. **Peers:** Think about your friends. What differences can you name in how each pays attention?

Comments: The school psychologist is a good resource for information on Attention Deficit Hyperactivity Disorder. Some students need quiet in order to study. What is your best way to work?

Extended Activities:

1. Have your students write the ideal conditions they need for doing work which requires concentration.
2. What do they do if the conditions aren't ideal?
3. How do they cope?

Lesson 7:   Ignoring Distractions

1. What is distracting me?

2. What do I need to do to keep working?

A. Ignore

B. Move

C. Ask the other person to stop.

3. Keep working.

CLASSROOM SKILLS

Lesson 8: Interrupting

Objective: Students will participate in class discussions without interrupting.

Materials Needed: None.

Establish the Need: Read the following story and discuss.

Interrupting

Mindy, Jeff, and Danny were on the nominating committee. Mindy was talking to Jeff and Danny about the class elections. Mindy said, "I want Amanda to win. She would make the best class president." Jeff said, "Yeah, yeah. Say, what did you think of that football game, Danny?" "Yeah, those Broncos really stomped the Vikings, didn't they?" Mindy said, "Say, we are supposed to be talking about...." "The Broncos made a cool pass in the fourth quarter that sealed the game! Did you see it?" said Danny. "You interrupted me! And we're supposed to be taking care of the elections," said Mindy.

1. Why was Mindy frustrated?
2. How do you feel when you are interrupted?

Procedures:

Step 1:　Model the skill:

Model using "Think Aloud" strategies—taking turns talking without interrupting.

1. Listen to the other person.
2. Wait until the person stops talking.
3. Take my turn talking.
4. Stay on the topic.

Step 2:　Role play with feedback:

Divide your class in groups of 5 or 6. Assign topics to be discussed with the specific direction that students must use "think aloud" strategies for interrupting. Rotate and give feedback.

Step 3:　Transfer training

A. **School:** Ask another teacher to reinforce strategies for not interrupting for the next two weeks.

B. **Home/Community:** At the next family dinner your assignment is to discuss something with your family without interrupting.

C. **Peers:** Have your students monitor their talking with friends for the day. Do they listen or do they interrupt?

Comments: Are interrupters good listeners?

Extended Activities:

1. Ask your students to design games based on listening without interrupting, i.e., only the person holding the chalk can talk and then pass the chalk.

2. Write a poem describing how you feel when you are listened to. How you feel when you are interrupted.

Lesson 8:   Interrupting

1. Listen to the other person.

2. Wait until the person stops talking.

3. Take my turn talking.

4. Stay on the topic.

CLASSROOM SKILLS

Lesson 9: Cooperative Working with Others

Objective: Students will work with peers to complete a task.

Materials Needed: Materials for the task of your choice. It could be an art project, class presentation, chapter outline, or map activity.

Establish the Need: Read the following story and discuss.

Butterfly Demise

Denise, Gretchen, Andy, and Joe were given the task of working together to make a replica of the stages of a butterfly—from larva, to chrysalis, to a butterfly. They agreed to meet at Denise's house to make the paper mache models. Andy was to bring the paint, Joe the paper, and Gretchen the models. They all gathered with their materials, except Andy forgot the paint. The project was due the next day.

1. What happens in a work group when all of the individuals do not do their parts?
2. What are some things necessary for groups to work together?

Procedures:

Step 1:   Model the skill:

Model using "Think Aloud" strategies—working cooperatively.

1. What do I need to bring?
2. Decide who does what.
3. Listen and share ideas.
4. Work until you are done.

Step 2:   Role play with feedback:

Assign your students to work in groups of 4 or 6 to complete a task you have determined. Give a due date. Rotate and give feedback for working cooperatively.

Step 3:   Transfer training

A. **School:** Ask a PE teacher to reinforce cooperative working with others.

B. **Home/Community:** Ask someone at home to help you with a task. Use cooperative working strategies.

C. **Peers:** Plan a social activity for class, emphasizing cooperative working.

Comments: More people are fired from jobs because they lack the ability to get along than from the lack of a job skill. Cooperative working is a lifelong skill.

Extended Activities:

1. List some of the things that require cooperative working in order for them to be accomplished.
2. Discuss how cooperative working is needed to get a bill passed in Congress.

Lesson 9:　Cooperative Working with Others

1. What do I need to bring?

2. Decide who does what.

3. Listen and share ideas.

4. Work until you are done.

CLASSROOM SKILLS

Lesson 10: Taking Notes

Objective: Students will take notes of a teacher presentation to study for a test.

Materials Needed: Brief presentation for which you have already identified the key points.

Establish the Need: Discuss the following:

No one can remember everything that has been said. That's why you need to take effective notes. You can't write down everything the teacher says, so you have to decide the important parts to write down. How do you decide that? Take notes about any name, date, or event you may need to remember. Also, take notes about lists of things, main points or steps to a task, or anything emphasized by the teacher.

Procedures:

Step 1: Model the skill:

Model using "Think Aloud" strategies—taking notes.

1. Have writing materials.
2. Listen for important points.
3. Write important details/information.
4. No need to write in full sentences.

Step 2: Role play with feedback:

Present the lecture you have prepared. When you are finished, outline on the board—with class input—what were the important items to be included in the class notes. Collect your students' notes to review and write feedback.

Step 3: Transfer training

A. **School:** Team with some other teachers to teach/reinforce note-taking skills. Practice with the students.

B. **Home/Community:** List some times, other than school, when you may want to take notes.

C. **Peers:** In groups of three, have your students share with each other some note-taking strategies.

Comments: Discuss what is relevant versus nonrelevant information. Give examples of each.

Extended Activities:

1. Arrange for a speaker to come to your class. Have your students take notes of the presentation and compare the content of their notes.

2. Give directions on how to get to a certain point in town. Have your students read from their notes to see if they wrote enough information to get there.

Lesson 10: Taking Notes

1. Have writing materials.

2. Listen. Is this important?

3. Write important details/information.

4. No need to write in full sentences.

CLASSROOM SKILLS

Lesson 11: Taking Tests

Objective: Students will prepare for and successfully respond to a test.

Materials Needed: A test that you select which is unfamiliar to students.

Establish the Need: Read and discuss the following story entitled "The Test."

Cody had a big biology test tomorrow, but his favorite programs were on TV tonight. He had been too busy with soccer, swim team, and scouts over the weekend to read the chapter. He knew he should study for the test, but he was so tired. He decided to watch just a little TV and then study.... Cody awakened in the morning when his mom turned on the kitchen light. He had fallen asleep watching TV and his mother had covered him with a blanket.

1. Is Cody going to be ready for the test?
2. How do you study for a test?

Procedures:

Step 1:   Model the skill:

Model using "Think Aloud" strategies—preparing for and taking tests.

1. Am I ready?
2. Breathe deeply.
3. Read the directions.
4. Answer the ones I know right away.
5. Check the clock for the remaining time.
6. Check to see if all items are answered.

Step 2:   Role play with feedback:

Hand out a test to your students. Tell them to take test using the "Think Aloud" strategies.

Step 3:   Transfer training

A. **School:** Ask other teachers to reinforce test-taking strategies.

B. **Home/Community:** Send home some test-taking tips (on the next page) and ask the parents to review with their children.

C. **Peers:** In groups of four, have your students share their ways of preparing for and taking tests.

Comments: See test-taking tips on page 119.

Extended Activities:

1. Teach your students that it is wise to prepare a little every day for a test. Do not wait until the last minute.
2. Lead a discussion with your students on how successful athletes would not be in the Olympics if they didn't prepare daily.
3. Name various kinds of tests. Are they all in school?
4. Have your students study using a tape recorder. The students read the material into the tape recorder, then they read it again leaving parts out, allowing wait time before giving the answer. They can listen and respond to the tape while bike riding, rollerblading, mowing the lawn, doing dishes and so forth.

Lesson 11: Taking Tests

1. Am I ready?

2. Breathe deeply.

3. Read the directions.

4. Answer the ones I know right away.

5. Check the clock for the time remaining.

6. Check to see if all items are answered.

CLASSROOM SKILLS

Lesson 12: Focusing on School

Objective: Students will prioritize their interests and determine what is needed to focus energy on success in school.

Materials Needed: None.

Establish the Need: List on the board or paper—with student input—all the events, organizations, sports, clubs, and sources of entertainment your students might want to enjoy. Beside each item record the time each activity might take in a day. List the obligations/necessities: school, eating, sleeping, and the time spent in those. Help your students to see that time is precious, and we need to decide how we wish to spend it.

Procedures:

Step 1: Model the skill:

Model using "Think Aloud" strategies—prioritizing your interests/needs/obligations within a time frame.

1. What are my obligations? At school? At home? To a friend?
2. How much time do I need for each?
3. What other activities do I want to do?
4. Can I fit those into my available time?

Step 2: Role play with feedback:

In groups of four, have your students list, prioritize, and figure the time needed for all activities in one day.

Step 3: Transfer training

A. **School:** Ask all of your students to figure how much time they need to spend outside of school to be successful at school.

B. **Home/Community:** How much time do you need to allot for family obligations? Chores?

C. **Peers:** In groups, have your students determine how much time they wish to spend and how much time is realistic to spend with friends.

Comments: Adolescents often have many obligations and a strong need for peer approval.

Extended Activities:

1. Have your students design or buy a small day planner. Teach them how to write down and prioritize the things they need to get done in one day.
2. Have them decide what they want to be doing in five years and prioritize what they need to do to achieve their goals.

Lesson 12: Focusing on School

1. What are my obligations? At school? At home? To a friend?

2. How much time does each take?

3. What other activities do I want to do?

4. Can I fit those into my available time?

CLASSROOM SKILLS

Lesson 13: Seeking Positive Attention From Peers

Objective: Students will learn how to seek peer attention in appropriate ways.

Materials Needed: None.

Establish the Need: Discuss the need for attention. Everyone wants to be noticed or recognized.

How you seek attention will help determine who your friends are, as well as affect how adults perceive you. Read and discuss the stories on the next page, "Sue—Respecting Her Peers and Friend" plus "Steve—The Pest."

Procedures:

Step 1: Model the skill:

Model using "Think Aloud" strategies—seeking positive peer attention.

1. Make eye contact. Say peer's name.
2. Be friendly and polite.
3. Begin a conversation.
4. If I meet with resistance, walk away and maybe try again.

Helpful Hints: Seeking positive attention takes patience and respect.

Step 2: Role play with feedback:

A. Role play seeking positive attention at lunch.

B. For contrast: role play inappropriate behavior to get attention: hitting, bugging, pestering, name calling, gossiping, and so forth.

Step 3: Transfer training

A. **School:** Say, "Hi" and "Can I sit next to you at lunch?" Wait for reply.

B. **Home/Community:** You see someone you would like to talk to at the mall. Make eye contact, smile, and be friendly.

C. **Peers:** Invite someone to study with you.

Comments: If you respect others, you will not force your behaviors or actions on them.

Golden Rule: Treat others as you would like to be treated.

Extended Activities:

1. Discuss: What happens to people when they violate other people's space or intimidate others? How do popular students seek positive attention from their peers?

2. Have your students write their own stories, using fictitious names, demonstrate seeking positive and negative attention. Discuss the stories.

Friendship Skills

Sue—Respecting Your Peers and Friends

Sue was a well-liked seventh grader. She was active in sports and band. Whenever she wanted to talk to her classmates, she would smile and say "hello" and ask how their day was going. She wasn't nosy or pushy and didn't get involved in gossip or rumors. Whenever she talked to others, she showed them respect. When she sat behind someone, she would politely tap that person on the shoulder if she wanted to know something. Students could talk to her because she would listen.

1. What kind of qualities did Sue have? (Respectful, good listener, polite.)
2. Does she know how to get people's attention the right way?
3. Does she seek others out or do they seek her out?
4. Would you be comfortable trying to get her attention?

Steve—The Pest

Steve was a rather small, insecure eighth grader who loved to bug the girls. He didn't have very many boys for friends. His mother had died from cancer. Last week he did something very unusual. He cut his hair very short and got an earring. He told everyone he was going to quit school after this year. He also got in trouble with the law and started ignoring his teachers. He started bugging the girls even more!

1. What do you think caused the sudden change in Steve?
2. Should someone in his class say something to Steve?
3. Should a counselor approach Steve?
4. What do you think Steve is saying with his behavior?
5. What do you think Steve is feeling?
6. Could Steve get his needs or wants met another way? How?

Lesson 13: Seeking Positive Attention From Peers

1. Make eye contact. Say your peer's name.

2. Be friendly and polite.

3. Begin a conversation.

4. If I meet with resistance, walk away and maybe try again.

FRIENDSHIP SKILLS

Lesson 14: Joining in a Group or Clique

Friendship Skills (side tab)

Objective: Students will learn how to ask to join a group or clique in an appropriate way.

Materials Needed: None.

Establish the Need: Read and discuss the stories on the next page: "The Tree Amigos" and "Billy—Small but Smart."

Procedures:

Step 1: Model the skill:

Model using "Think Aloud" strategies.

1. How do I approach the group or clique?
2. Choose a good time.
3. Ask if I can join the group.
4. Wait for an answer.
5. Choose something else to do if the answer is "no."

Gender Differences: Boys may be more apt to join sports, gangs, or clubs, whereas girls often belong to cliques. Boys may find size and strength a prerequisite to belonging. The secret is to find a group which accepts you and one with which you are comfortable. Girls may find it tough to be accepted by the group they desire. An idea for acceptance is to invite one or two members of the group to do something with you. Get to know them individually before approaching the entire group. True friends accept you as you are.

Step 2: Role play with feedback:

A. Have your students form groups and take turns asking to join. Observe and give feedback.

B. Have them practice being rejected and making another choice of what else to do.

Helpful Hints: No one ever goes through life without a number of rejections. How do rejections make you feel? Who might you talk to about your feelings?

Step 3: Transfer training

A. **School:** Practice joining a group after school.

B. **Home/Community:** Practice joining a group in your neighborhood or at your church youth group.

C. **Peers:** Practice having someone new join your group. Why do we try to exclude people from groups?

Comments: During adolescence, groups and cliques seem to be the norm. This is a period where teens who are considered too different may be shunned. This is an excellent time to provide tolerance training for your students to assist them to tolerate personal differences of all kinds.

Extended Activities:

1. Pick a TV show that addresses this issue—*Friends, Simpsons*, or any current TV show. Why is it important to belong and be accepted? Name some ways adolescents try to be accepted.

2. Have your school counselor or a guest counselor do an activity on tolerance.

The Three Amigos

Three girls—Monique, Brandi, and Megan—were best of friends. They went everywhere together. They were a solid threesome when they were in elementary school. However, all that changed after they went to middle school. All of a sudden they started to squabble, argue, and exclude each other. One day, Brandi transferred to a private school. She didn't call or talk to Monique or Megan for several weeks.

Can you guess what happened to Brandi? Mystery question!

A. Her parents wanted her to go to a new school.

B. Brandi wanted to go to a new school.

C. Her boyfriend attended this school.

D. You fill in an answer.

Billy—Small but Smart

Billy always wanted to play basketball, but he was very small for his age and not very athletic. However, Billy was friends with most of the players on the team. Billy tried out for basketball in school, but he didn't make the team. One day he had an idea. He knew he wouldn't make the team, but he thought about being a team manager. He waited anxiously outside the gym door. The coach called Billy into the locker area and all the players agreed to have Billy as their team manager. Billy was happy because he could still hang around his friends. The way Billy looked at it, he may be small in seventh grade, but what about high school? He could be really tall and talented by then. Sometimes you cannot have things right when you want them, but that doesn't mean you can't choose something else you would like to do.

1. What kind of qualities did Billy have?

2. How did he try to "fit in?"

3. Did he give up?

4. What kind of outlook did Billy have? Was it realistic? Could you do that?

5. Would you have done things differently if you were Billy?

Lesson 14: Joining in a Group or Clique

1. How do I approach the group or clique?

2. Choose a good time.

3. Ask if I can join.

4. Wait for an answer.

5. Find something else to do if the answer is "no."

FRIENDSHIP SKILLS

Dennis Hanken, Ed.S. and Judith Kennedy, Ed.S.

Lesson 15: How to Survive the Social Triangle

Objective: Students will be able to interact in a group containing three or more.

Materials Needed: Picture of a triangle.

Establish the Need: What does the effect of three people have on a relationship and feeling left out? It seems that two people can get along, but if you add a third, then there is competition for attention. One person inevitably feels left out. Read and discuss the story, "The Three Musketeers," on the next page.

Procedures:

Step 1: Model the skill:

Model using "Think Aloud" strategies

1. What do I want in a friend?
2. Am I feeling left out?
3. What are my choices?
   A. Establish ground rules.
   B. Talk to my friends about how I feel.
   C. Find someone else to do things with.

Gender Differences: This skill is mostly for girls. Girls may play one against the other. Triangles can be tough to handle for adolescent girls. Parents and teachers may need to listen and have empathy.

Step 2: Role play with feedback:

A. In groups of three, have your students role play appropriate ways of handling the triangle using "Think Aloud" strategies.
B. In class discuss what breaks up triangles.

Helpful Hints: If your students are aware of how triangles make people feel, they will be better able to deal with them.

Step 3: Transfer training

A. **School:** Practice this skill when you have more than one friend at an activity or during lunch.
B. **Home/Community:** Practice this skill in your neighborhood or outside activity.
C. **Peers:** Set up some ground rules with two of your best friends. Talk about past problems and how to prevent them.

Helpful Hints: Talk about some issues that you had in elementary school. How did you resolve issues and problems?

Extended Activities:

1. Discuss the *roles* each person plays in the triangle. There is usually a leader, a follower, and a peacemaker. What happens if there are two leaders? (Use the triangle to demonstrate.)
2. Discuss: What are the qualities of a friend? What do you expect from a friend? *Can* you live up to your own expectations? *Do* you live up to your expectations? Make a list of do's and don'ts for being a friend.
3. Discuss having more than one friend. Does that complicate the relationships? Why? Look at other groups or triangles. Do they last? When you involve boys in the friendship, is the result the same?

The Three Musketeers

Beth, Amanda, and Sara were the three musketeers; they did everything together. Their parents expected them to be lifelong pals since they were almost like sisters. They had been friends since kindergarten. A strange thing happened during the last part of seventh grade. Beth started dating, Amanda became a cheerleader, and Sara was wondering what happened. Sara started looking around for other friends. Beth, Amanda, and Sara still liked each other, but the closeness they once had seemed to be fading. They started finding excuses for not being with each other. Sara even started her own little clique. Amanda and Beth didn't like this a bit. Amanda and Beth eventually merged with several other girls and excluded Sara.

1. Do you think Sara, Amanda, and Beth ever had ground rules?
2. What really broke up the triangle?
3. Do you think Sara will ever join Amanda and Beth in their group?
4. What do you think Sara was feeling?
5. Do people grow apart? Is that okay?
6. How might Sara, Amanda, and Beth have handled this differently?

Lesson 15: How to Survive the Triangle

1. What do I want in a friend?

2. Am I feeling left out?

3. What are my choices?

   A. Establish ground rules.

   B. Talk to my friends about how I feel.

   C. Find someone else to do things with.

FRIENDSHIP SKILLS

Lesson 16: Gossip and Put-downs

Friendship Skills

Objective: Students will be able to verbally interact with peers without resorting to gossip and negative put-downs.

Materials Needed: Journals.

Establish the Need: Define gossip: often groundless rumor of a personal, sensational, or intimate nature, idle talk. Put-downs: insulting remarks which may make the receiving person feel worthless and sad. Examples:

1. Amanda, a sixth grader, was always spreading gossip about two girls in her class. She didn't like them, and it made her feel good to see these girls try to deny the accusations. One of the girls found out that Amanda was spreading the gossip. She confronted Amanda. What do you think she should say to Amanda? What do you think Amanda's reply will be? What is Amanda's goal?

2. Megan wore very nice clothes to school. Her clothes were always the best and latest in fashion. When she saw girls in her class who wore something she didn't approve of, she would make fun of them and criticize them. Nobody would stand up to Megan. One day, however, a new girl told her it was none of her business what she wore to school. Do you think this changed Megan's behavior? Does she have the right to tell people they are wearing the wrong clothes? Why do you think Megan does this?

3. Ask your students to relate situations (without names) where gossip or put-downs hurt someone.

4. Read and discuss the fable, "The Eagle, the Wildcat, and the Sow," on page 52.

Procedures:

Step 1: Model the skill:

Model using "Think Aloud" strategies—Reacting to gossip and put-downs.

1. Am I offended by the remarks of another?
2. What can I do?
   A. Ignore.
   B. Speak up with a strong voice, confront without put-downs.
   C. Avoid the person making the remarks.
   D. Walk away.
   E. Get a mediator.

Gender Differences: When boys get into this, there can be physical fights, pushing, shoving, and name calling. It seems after the incident is over, it is more quickly forgotten. However, girls may have more trouble letting go of slights, getting their friends involved, and holding grudges. Sometimes these disagreements need adult intervention before being resolved. Parents need to be aware of these issues so they can help their children deal with them.

Dennis Hanken, Ed.S. and Judith Kennedy, Ed.S.

Step 2:   Role play with feedback:

Role play in groups of three handling gossip and put-downs. Give feedback.

Helpful Hints: Teaching assertiveness may help students handle this.

Step 3:   Transfer training

A. **School:** Students should refrain from gossip and put-downs. Give two positive "put up" comments each day.

B. **Home/Community:** Journal. Are put-downs common at home? How might you react when parents or siblings put you down? Confront appropriately.

C. **Peers:** True friends do not put-down or gossip about each other. Friends accept you for who you are. Most friends defend against gossip. Write what you think are essential qualities in a friendship.

Comments: Many schools have a philosophy that negative comments are not tolerated. Violence begins with gestures of ridicule, gossip, and criticism. The time to stop violence is when it is beginning.

Extended Activities: Try the "gossip game." Whisper something in one student's ear, have that student repeat it to the next, and so forth until it has gone all the way around the room. Then have the last person say what he or she heard out loud. Is it what you said in the first place? Human nature causes us to change things slightly between hearing and repeating something, not out of malice, but because of the way we remember and interpret information.

The Eagle, the Wildcat, and the Sow

An eagle chose the top branches of an old oak tree for her nest and hatched her young there. A wildcat had selected the hollow trunk of the same tree for her den where she would raise her little ones. Down among the roots of the old oak a sow had burrowed a hole where she planned to raise her piglets in comfort.

For some time all three families lived peacefully in the old oak, until the wildcat took a notion to start gossiping about her neighbors.

"Neighbor," she whispered to the eagle, "as you know I have the highest respect for that old sow down below. But if she keeps rooting under this tree, the whole thing will come crashing down someday. That's probably what she has in mind so she can feed our babies to her litter."

Needless to say, the mother eagle was worried. She was so disturbed that she did not dare to leave her nest to go in search of food. Meanwhile, the gossiping wildcat visited the sow.

"Mrs. Sow," she whispered, "I'm no gossip, as you know, but if I were you, I wouldn't leave home today. I overheard that eagle upstairs telling her children they were going to have pork for supper."

So the eagle stayed in her nest and the sow remained with her little pigs. But the wildcat sneaked off every night and got food for her kittens, while her neighbors lived in distrust of each other.

It is possible that both families would have starved to death had not the wildcat made the mistake of getting caught in a hunter's snare, and the sow and the eagle became reunited in caring for the abandoned kittens.

1. Who is hurt by gossip?
2. Name some examples from the news where gossip has hurt someone.
3. How can gossip be damaging to the person who gossips?

Dennis Hanken, Ed.S. and Judith Kennedy, Ed.S.

Lesson 16: Gossip and Put-downs

1. **Am I offended by the remarks of another?**

2. **What can I do?**

   A. **Ignore.**

   B. **Speak up with a strong voice, confront without put-downs.**

   C. **Avoid the person making the remarks.**

   D. **Walk away.**

   E. **Get a mediator.**

FRIENDSHIP SKILLS

Lesson 17: Apologizing

Objective: Students will be able to apologize sincerely for doing something wrong.

Materials Needed: None.

Establish the Need: Some people have no problem apologizing while others have a hard time saying "I'm sorry." It is important to be sincere when we apologize. Discuss this as a class. Talk about different situations that require an apology—gossip, rumors, injury, embarrassment, breaking something, and so forth. Read and discuss the story, "I Made a Mistake—I'm sorry, Please Forgive Me," on the following page.

Procedures:

Step 1:   Model the skill:

Using "Think Aloud" strategies, model apologizing for borrowing a CD from another student and losing it.

1. Establish eye contact.
2. Did I do something wrong?
3. How should I apologize?
   A. Say "I am sorry for...." (Be specific.)
   B. Replace the object broken or lost.
4. Apologize as soon as possible.

Helpful Hints: Sometimes it is difficult to admit that you made a mistake. If you put yourself in the other person's place, it may help you see that an apology is necessary. Think of it as relationship glue.

Step 2:   Role play with feedback:

Have your students pair up and practice apologizing and also receiving an apology in a gracious manner.

Gender Differences: Boys sometimes find it more difficult to apologize. Girls may prefer to apologize to avoid a physical fight. Sometimes girls don't forgive and forget. Verbalizing and forgiving are crucial for one's own health and that of the relationship.

Step 3:   Transfer training

A. **School:** If you have a friend or teacher you have wronged, this would be a good opportunity to apologize.

B. **Home/Community:** Discuss how your family handles apologizing.

C. **Peers:** Have you had a fallout recently with a friend that isn't resolved yet? Is there a need for you to apologize?

Comments: Taking the first step in apologizing is sometimes the most difficult. If the friendship is important to you, an apology is a step toward healing the damage.

Extended Activities: Should teachers apologize to students? We all have choices and opportunities to make relationships better. The true test of friendship is how you resolve conflict. Your friendship can either become better or fade with conflict.

I Made a Mistake—I'm Sorry, Please Forgive Me

John was an eighth grader who was kind of restless. His mother called him a bull in a china closet. One day he was running in the hallway and ran smack into a teacher. He almost knocked the teacher over and managed to send three books to the floor. The teacher was angry with John. John said, "I shouldn't have been running in the hallway. I am really sorry." The teacher felt like John was sorry for what he had done, and it was an accident, so he didn't report him to the principal.

1. Do you know someone who has trouble taking responsibility for his or her behavior?

2. How does saying "I'm sorry" help?

Lesson 17: Apologizing

1. Establish eye contact.

2. Did I do something wrong?

3. How should I apologize?

    A. Say "I am sorry for...." (Be specific.)

    B. Replace the object I lost or broke.

4. Apologize as soon as possible.

FRIENDSHIP SKILLS

Lesson 18: Responding to Teasing and Name Calling

Objective: Students will ignore or change the subject when they are teased or respond in another appropriate manner.

Materials Needed: Paper for drawing, pencil.

Establish the Need: Sometimes we tease family members and close friends, perhaps because it is a way of making "light" of certain issues. It is not intended to hurt others. Teasing to hurt someone is wrong. It not only hurts someone's feelings, but it makes the teaser look small in the eyes of others. Read the stories on the next page. It is a fine line between teasing in fun and being mean. The only way to tell whether the teasing is in fun or meanness is to evaluate the effect it has on the other person. It is best not to tease at all unless you have an understanding relationship with the person you are teasing. Read and discuss the stories on the next page entitled "Teasing the Wrong Way" and "Who Did It?"

Procedures:

Step 1:   Model the skill:

Model using "Think Aloud" strategies—

(1) Am I being teased? (2) Choices. A. Ignore. B. Walk away. C. Change the subject. D. Respond by saying, "I don't like being teased," in a strong/assertive voice.

Helpful Hints: At this age, students are very sensitive about their physical appearance, (size, weight, looks, hair, etc.).

Step 2:   Role play with feedback:

A. Have your students pair up and role play responding to teasing, using "Think Aloud" strategies.

B. Have them write a cartoon strip with captions illustrating this lesson.

Step 3:   Transfer training

A. **School:** When others tease you in PE, the hallways, or after school, have a plan on how to respond.

B. **Home/Community:** Have your students talk about the teasing that goes on at home with siblings and parents.

C. **Peers:** When your best friend teases you, do you get mad? What is the best way to handle it when it happens every day?

Comments: Teasing can be a form of flirting. Being aware of the feelings of others is very important!!

Extended Activities:

1. Discuss: An appropriate response if we tease and hurt someone is, "I'm sorry, I didn't mean to hurt you."

2. Journal about what areas are sensitive for you. These are areas that are more vulnerable to teasing. They may include physical attributes as well as personal characteristics.

3. Have a class discussion on why people tease.

Teasing the Wrong Way

Bob and John, both eighth graders, had been best buddies, but lately they didn't hang out as much as they used to. When they did see each other, they were rude and mean. The teasing was getting ugly and out of control. One day it escalated to the point of becoming physical. Eventually they just didn't like each other any more; they had become rather distant. They couldn't even be nice to each other any more.

1. Did Bob and John lose respect for each other, and teasing became a way of getting back at each other? Discuss.
2. What happened to their friendship?
3. Would communication help?
4. How could Bob and John have resolved their difficulties earlier?

Who Did It?

Annie, Joan, Shelia, and Bethany were good friends and sixth graders. They liked teasing each other. Joan seemed to be the instigator of the team and teased the others about anything. They seemed to take turns. One day Shelia found rocks in her book locker. All three of her friends knew the combination to her locker. Annie said Bethany did it. Shelia suspected Joan because she did so much teasing.

1. Who really did it? Can you guess? The answer is below.
2. Is teasing okay if everyone is enjoying it?

Annie—She knew Joan would be blamed.
Annie accused Bethany to focus the blame off her.

Lesson 18: Responding to Teasing and Name Calling

1. Am I being teased?

2. Choices.

A. Ignore.

B. Walk away.

C. Change the subject.

D. Respond by saying, "I don't like being teased," in a strong/assertive voice.

FRIENDSHIP SKILLS

Lesson 19: Making and Keeping a Friend

Objective: Students will be able to learn how to be a friend in an appropriate way.

Materials Needed: Sociogram, to discover which children don't seem to have friends. Journal. (Sociogram: Have each student write anonymously on paper which five students in the class they like best. Tabulate the answers to see which students are not selected.)

Establish the Need: What is a friend? List the general characteristics that define what you would look for in a friend. Does the phrase, "Friends forever," hold true? Read and discuss the stories entitled "A Day on Venus" and "True Friends" on page 61.

Procedures:

Step 1:   Model the skill:

Model using "Think Aloud" strategies—making a new friend.

1. Smile and say "Hello" whenever you can.
2. Start a conversation and act interested in the other person.
3. Ask that person to come to an activity, walk home, or come over to your house after school or on a weekend.
4. If you have mutual interests and like each other, keep promoting trust and interest.

Helpful Hints: Once you get to know someone you will either want to be around that person more or you will discover that you don't have much in common. It is important to accept people for who they are and don't try to change them.

Step 2:   Role play with feedback:

A. Role play in twos how to make a new friend. Discuss your feelings and give feedback to each other.

B. Discuss: What happens when the friendship doesn't work?

Step 3:   Transfer training

A. **School:** Engage another student who you would like for a friend and see what happens. Report back to the teacher. Discuss the results.

B. **Home/Community:** Try to find someone new and friendly in the neighborhood or someplace where you hang out.

C. **Peers:** When you're at a game or activity, ask to sit by someone or go somewhere after the activity. Sound interested in that person and what he or she likes to do.

Comments: It is fun to meet new people and learn about them, their family, and friends. Talk about how some friends follow you around and want you all to themselves. Remember, you can't force friendship.

Extended Activities:

1. Discuss the differences between friends and best friends. How about the differences between the people you know and your friends? What is a friend, or best friend? How many best friends do you have? Make a list and then average for the class how

many friends and best friends people have. Which is longer? Why? Thought for the Day: One way to express that you care about another person is to really listen when that person talks.

2. Have your students break into small groups of two or four with their goal being to talk until they discover things they have in common, i.e., food they like, TV shows, activities, color, and so forth. This shows students that they are more alike than different.

3. Journal the qualities you have that make you a good friend. Are there areas you could improve?

4. As a class, list all the qualities that make a person a good friend.

A Day on Venus

Mallow was a Martian who landed on Venus one day. While he was looking around, he met a person from Venus called Scorpe. They got to talking and they found they had a lot in common. They started to really like each other. One day Mallow got a message from Mars, "Please come home, you are way past due." But Mallow, even though he wasn't at home, felt he found a pleasant place to stay, as well as a good friend. This was something he didn't have on Mars. Scorpe kept saying "You're my favorite Martian."

What would Mallow do?
  A. Fly to earth and settle in LA.
  B. Stay in Venus and be friends with Scorpe.
  C. Fly back to Mars.
  D. Explain your answer!

True Friends

Bob and John, eighth graders, were the best of friends since the fourth grade. John, however, found a girlfriend and spent a lot of time with her. Bob still liked John, but he was getting jealous and frustrated. Bob thought about his options, and he decided that the best thing to do was to just enjoy his time when John was available.

1. Do you think Bob made the right decision?

2. How do you think John felt?

3. What are some other ways to work out sharing time with friends?

Lesson 19: Making and Keeping a Friend

1. Smile and say "Hello" whenever you can.

2. Start a conversation and act interested in the other person.

3. Ask that person to come to an activity, walk home, or come over to your house after school or on the weekend.

4. If you have mutual interests and like each other, keep promoting trust and interest.

FRIENDSHIP SKILLS

Lesson 20: Respecting Others' Property

Objective: Students will learn to respect others' property and respect their rights.

Materials Needed: None.

Establish the Need: Name your most prized possession. Would you let your best friend borrow it? If we don't respect the property of others, can we expect them to respect ours? Discuss trading and borrowing, i.e., girls with clothes and makeup and boys with games, hats, and sports equipment. What are the risks in lending things? Read and discuss the stories on the next page, "What Should I Do Next?" and "Honesty and Truthfulness."

Procedures:

Step 1:   Model the skill:

Model using "Think Aloud" strategies.

1. Did I borrow or use someone's property?

2. If it is borrowed, I should treat it like it was mine.

3. If I damage or lose it, I should replace it.

4. If I find something that is valuable, I should try to find the owner.

Gender Differences: This is the age when girls borrow clothes and other personal things. Boys trade and borrow games, hats, and toys. Sometimes parents buy expensive gifts. Should these be lent out?

Step 2:   Role play with feedback:

A. Role play with your students how to respect the property of others or school property.

B. Role play destroying someone's property. Should you be held accountable and replace the item? Discuss.

Step 3:   Transfer training

A. **School:** You need to borrow a calculator for math class. It falls out of your locker and breaks. What is the first thing that you do?

B. **Home/Community:** Do you respect your sibling's property and the privacy of his or her room?

C. **Peers:** Ask your friend to borrow a video game. Should you lend that person's game to someone else?

Comments: Discuss trashing a motel and other means of destroying public property, i.e., vandalism, graffiti.

Extended Activities:

1. Discuss damaging property. Ask for stories from your students. Should you protect a friend who knowingly destroyed property? Is there a lack of respect for the property of others in our society? Discuss.

2. Have a class meeting and discuss ideas for decreasing damage that people do to the school. Write out the ideas and present them to the school board.

What Should I Do Next?

Jill was walking down the hall and found a purse that belonged to someone in school. There was a lot of money and jewelry in it. Jill thought that the person who lost the purse would probably be very upset. It was tempting to just take it home or think "finders keepers." But then she thought how she would feel if she lost something. Wouldn't she want to have someone return it? Jill turned the purse into the office, and they found the owner. Jill felt very good about what she did.

1. What temptations did Jill have to deal with?
2. Do you think most teenagers would do what Jill did?
3. Should Jill get a reward?

Honesty and Truthfulness

David was cruising the mall looking for his friends when the man walking in front of him dropped a twenty dollar bill. No one saw this but David. The man didn't know. David quickly put his foot over the money and looked around to see if anyone else had witnessed what he had. No one had! The twenty was his!! Or was it?

1. How would you end this scenario?
2. What would you do?
3. What if you had lost the twenty dollar bill?
4. Are you sure no one saw the incident?

Lesson 20: Respecting Others' Property

1. Did I borrow or use someone's property?

2. If it is borrowed, I should treat it like it was mine.

3. If I damage or lose it, I should replace it.

4. If I find something that is valuable, I should try to find the owner.

FRIENDSHIP SKILLS

Lesson 21: Should I Join a Clique, Gang, or Club?

Objective: Students will be able to make good choices about joining groups.

Materials Needed: None.

Establish the Need: List the clubs in your town that students can join. Define clique, gang, and club. Why is there a need to join groups? Discuss why there is a strong human need to belong to any group that gives you identity and self-worth. Can belonging to a gang be a positive move? Read and discuss the story, "Sociable vs. Practical," on the next page.

Procedures:

Step 1:   Model the skill:

Model using "Think Aloud" strategies—joining a clique, gang, or club.

1. What do I know about the group?
2. Is this a group I would fit in?
3. Do I want to be associated with this group?
   A. Gangs—might have a negative impact. Are there drugs, weapons, violence?
   B. Cliques—might hurt others by ignoring their feelings and excluding them.
   C. Clubs—Should I join? What is the commitment?
4. Weigh all the facts.
5. Make the right choice.

Step 2:   Role play with feedback:

A. Have your students pick each group and role play joining them. Discuss the issues with friends, adults, and parents.
B. Role play being rejected by each group and discuss the results.

Gender Differences: Boys are more likely to join gangs and athletic groups. They seem to gravitate towards more competitive and aggressive groups. However, girls are also admitted to gangs to fulfill a role. Many of these students get into trouble with the law and do poorly in school. Students in athletic groups usually do better academically, but they may become egoistical if the sport isn't put in perspective. Girls may join social groups or sports. Most girls are not as aggressive as boys. Girls in cliques can be both positive and negative. Some cliques are vicious and rude, creating rumors and lies. Some cliques are just several girls who like each other as true friends.

Step 3:	Transfer training

A. **School:** Ask to join a club or ask to join a school-related group. Discuss results.

B. **Home/Community:** Ask to join a community sport team or group. Would you join a gang just to be cool?

C. **Peers:** Can a clique of five to six students be a support group? Peer pressure can overshadow good judgment.

Comments: Most people want to be popular and liked. Different groups can lead to different problems. It is important not to change the way you are just to fit in. It is important not to abandon your values to fit in with a group.

Extended Activities:

1. Ask your students, how many gangs exist in school? Do girls prefer to be in cliques? What if you don't belong to a clique or group? Is that bad?

2. Discuss the harmful effects of cliques.

3. Discuss people joining cults. Why do people join? What are they looking for?

4. Discuss clubs and organizations adults join. What are they looking for?

5. Why have people created towns and cities? What purposes do these fill?

Sociable vs. Practical

Karie was asked to join a very sociable—but rather exclusive—clique in her school. Karie was a mature seventh grader and new to this school. She asked around the school about what kind of a clique this was. Most of the answers were that these girls were gossip queens, rude, and very stuck-up. Karie decided to join the school chorus and didn't have time to be associated with this clique.

1. Did Karie make the right decision?
2. Karie was very smart to do what first?

Lesson 21: Should I Join a Clique, Gang, or Club

1. What do I know about the group?

2. Is this a group I would fit in?

3. Do I want to be associated with this group?

    A. Gangs—might have a negative impact. Are there drugs, weapons, violence?

    B. Cliques—might hurt others by ignoring their feelings and excluding them.

    C. Clubs—Should I join? What is the commitment?

4. Weigh all the facts.

5. Make the right choice.

FRIENDSHIP SKILLS

Lesson 22: Note Passing

Objective: Students will be able to make the right choice about writing notes, the content of notes, and when is an appropriate time to write them.

Materials Needed: Put an acceptable note on the board or overhead.

Establish the Need: Note passing is very common in middle school and high school, because friends aren't always in the same class. Note passing is okay when it is more informational and less harmful, and when it isn't done when you should be listening to the teacher or doing a school task. If you say something in a note that is harmful to someone and the note gets in the wrong hands, it can be disaster to both the person writing it and the person being named. Read and discuss the story, "Warning Signs," on the next page.

Procedures:

Step 1:   Model the skill:

Model using "Think Aloud" strategies.

1. Should I write the note?
2. Is this the time and the place?
3. Can I say it another way?

   A. In person.

   B. On the phone.

   C. Wait until another time.

4. Is it gossip or harmful to someone else?
5. Make the right choice.

Gender Differences: Girls are more apt to write notes than boys. Most of the time note writing is harmless and informative. It is a way of staying in touch with friends and classmates. Sometimes it is rude and careless of others' feelings. If a note gets into the wrong hands, it can cause you to lose friends and be the "scapegoat" or subject of gossip. Discuss scapegoat. Discuss what content should not be in notes.

Step 2:   Role play with feedback:

A. Have your students write notes using "Think Aloud" strategies. Notes need to be appropriate and written at the right time.

B. Have them role play writing thank you notes, or birthday or party invitations.

Helpful Hints: You write a note about how bad a teacher is to you. You try to pass it in the hallway and a teacher picks it up instead. She calls your parents. Discuss.

Friendship Skills

> **Step 3:   Transfer training**

A. **School:** Write a note to a teacher, telling your teacher how great it is to be in class.

B. **Home/Community:** Write a note to your parents, thanking them for something lately.

C. **Peers:** Write your best friend a "thank you" note for being a good friend.

Comments: Once you put something in writing and sign your name, you are committed to it. If you are writing notes during class and you miss information, whose problem is it?

Extended Activities:

1. Make a list of Do's and Don'ts for note writing and passing. Teachers should talk to classes about note writing, appropriate and inappropriate times, and content.

2. Write notes to pen pals, senior citizens in assisted living, or students in a lower grade.

3. Create a skit showing what a fiasco gossip can be in note writing and passing.

Warning Signs

Stephanie and Tara were the best of friends all through the seventh grade. Tara always wrote Stephanie notes about everything that was happening in school. However, Tara would also say something negative about her family and that she couldn't stand her math teacher. The notes were getting pretty nasty by the third quarter. Stephanie told Tara to "cool it" on the notes because someone else might see them. She suggested they talk on the phone. But Tara wouldn't listen. One day a note slipped out of Stephanie's back pack and the assistant principal found it. He talked to Tara and then he phoned her parents about the note.

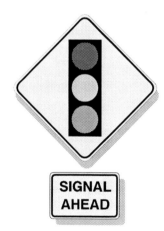

SIGNAL AHEAD

1. What do you think happened next?

2. Should Tara be more aware of note passing with inappropriate comments about teachers and parents?

3. Should Tara be responsible and be punished for her poor judgment?

4. Should Stephanie not read her notes until they are better and more positive?

5. How else might Tara handle her feelings about her family and teacher?

Lesson 22: Note Passing

1. Should I write the note?

2. Is this the time and place?

3. Can I say it another way?

   A. In person.

   B. On the phone.

   C. Wait until another time.

4. Is it gossip or harmful to someone else?

5. Make the right choice.

FRIENDSHIP SKILLS

Lesson 23: Girls and Boys in Adolescence—Recognizing the Differences in Making Friends

Friendship Skills

Objective: Students will recognize that girls and boys have different feelings and emotions.

Materials Needed: None.

Establish the Need: Make a list of some similar and different qualities of boys and girls. How do boys make friends? How do girls make friends?

Gender Differences: Feelings, emotions, and opinions can differ greatly between boys and girls. Girls experience adolescent growth approximately two years before boys. Boys' growth is more extended through and beyond adolescence. Girls may be taller and bigger at the onset of adolescence, but boys usually catch up. Physical changes, sexual urges, self-concept, race, school problems, values, morals, and families are all sources of differences and similarities throughout adolescence among and between genders. Dating and friendships between genders begin sooner for some than for others, and can be a source of tension. Read and discuss the story, "Finding a Common Interest," on the next page.

Procedures:

Step 1: Model the skill:

Model using "Think Aloud" strategies.

1. How am I different from a girl/boy?
2. How am I the same as a girl/boy?

Step 2: Role play with feedback:

A. Arrange students in groups with two boys and two girls. Discuss the *similarities* between the genders.

B. Have the same group discuss the *differences* between the genders.

Helpful Hints: Knowing that girls and boys not only act but think differently is important throughout life. The adolescent years help students discern qualities important to them and what traits they want in friendships and partnerships. Note: Girls often form friendships on sharing feelings, while boys form relationships on sharing experiences.

Step 3: Transfer training

A. **School:** Talk to a peer of a different gender to find similarities and differences. Be a good listener.

B. **Home/Community:** Make an effort to meet a different gender peer.

C. **Peers:** Invite a different gender peer to join you for a soda.

Extended Activity: Brainstorm, as a class, what are important qualities to have, (i.e., have the girls say what are important qualities for boys to have and vice versa.)

Finding a Common Interest

Kris had the biggest crush on John in the eighth grade, but wasn't able to "break the ice" with him. He didn't seem to be interested in her at all. Kris found out that John had an older brother, Bill, who ran around with Kris's best friend's brother, Kurt. They both played football on the high school team. Kris saw John one day alone at the mall. She finally got enough courage to ask him about Bill and Kurt. John went on and on about them. She listened to him for twenty minutes. John liked the way Kris listened and smiled. He finally was quiet and asked her if she wanted to walk home together. She said, "Yes".

1. Finding a common experience sometimes breaks the "ice."

2. Did Kris find a way to have John talk?

3. Having a plan doesn't always work, but knowing something about another person is one way to start.

4. Can this work with boy to boy or girl to girl?

Lesson 23: Girls and Boys in Adolescents— Recognizing the Differences in Making Friends

1. How am I different from girls/boys?

2. How am I the same as girls/boys?

3. Girls develop closeness through talking and sharing their feelings.

4. Boys tend to develop closeness through sharing experiences.

FRIENDSHIP SKILLS

Lesson 24: Respecting and Trusting Yourself Helps Others to Respect and Trust You

Objective: Students will be able to describe themselves, their strengths and weaknesses, and talk about what they like about themselves and what changes they need to make.

Materials Needed: Journals.

Establish the Need: Some people find it hard to list their own strengths and weaknesses. Why is that? Have your students draw lines on a paper to make quadrants. In the top left, put one's own perceived weaknesses; in the top right, one's strengths; in the bottom left, one's areas for improving; and in the bottom right, list the things others like about you. Read and discuss the story, "Change is Good," on the next page.

Procedures:

Step 1: Model the skill:

Model using "Think Aloud" strategies.

1. I like myself as I am.
2. Know my strengths and weaknesses.
3. Enjoy my time alone.
4. What do others like about me?

Step 2: Role play with feedback:

A. Get into small groups and list your strengths. Do others see these strengths?

B. Use the same groups to list your weaknesses. Do others see these traits?

C. List people who you think respect and trust you. Why do they trust and respect you? Discuss.

D. Have your students tell others what they like about each other.

Step 3: Transfer training

A. **School:** Journal. How many classmates really respect and trust you?

B. **Home/Community:** Do you respect and trust your parents? Why?

C. **Peers:** Does being popular with your peers mean that they trust and respect you?

Comments: Some friendships come and go. Which friendships last forever? If you like yourself, others are more likely to like your strengths and accept your weaknesses. Nobody is perfect. Sometimes you must overlook someone's faults to see the real person.

Extended Activities:

1. As an art project, have each person create a collage depicting their strengths, interests, and hobbies.

2. As a class project, make a collage with the students choosing one thing to represent themselves. Discuss how the uniqueness of each individual contributes to the group.

Change is Good

Jason was thinking one day about how much he had grown up last year. Some of the students he didn't like before seemed to be okay now in his mind and vice versa. What had happened? Jason had thought about all of his good qualities and some of his faults. He decided to change some of his behavior. He found that as he changed for the better, his circle of friends got larger. What a deal! He has more friends than he ever had. He liked himself more because he was able to change. Jason found that more students liked him now.

Do we always have a choice to be a better person?

Students want to be around happy, fun, loving, positive peers.

It makes them feel better, too!

Can we decide to change things about our behavior?

Lesson 24: Respecting and Trusting Yourself Helps Others to Respect and Trust You

1. I like myself as I am.

2. Know my strengths and weaknesses.

3. Enjoy my time alone.

4. What do others like about me?

FRIENDSHIP SKILLS

Lesson 25: Showing Your Feelings

Objective: Students will identify and appropriately express feelings.

Materials Needed: Book: *Bridge Over Tabithia by Katherine Paterson*, Journals.

Establish the Need: Read *Bridge Over Tabithia* in class. Discuss how the characters showed their feelings toward each other. How are feelings shown after the death? Name other ways you have seen people show they care for each other. Elicit examples from your students. Name all the feelings in the story. How long is the story?

Procedures:

Step 1:   Model the skill:

Model using "Think Aloud" strategies—showing feelings appropriately.

1. What do I feel?
2. Why do I feel this way?
3. How can I express what I feel?
4. Choose an appropriate way.

Step 2:   Role play with feedback:

Create scenarios which elicit various feelings, i.e., school is closed for snow, your soccer team wins the tournament, your best friend moves away, a teacher accuses you of cheating on a test, a tough group of kids threaten to beat you up after school. Have your students act out your scenarios.

Step 3:   Transfer training

A. **School:** You study hard for a test, but do poorly on it. How do you feel? What do you do?

B. **Home/Community:** Your parents think you are too young to go to the all-school party. How do you feel?

C. **Peers:** The group you like is going to the mall. They haven't included you. How do you feel?

Comments: Teach your students that feelings are normal and healthy. We can't choose our feelings, but we can choose how we show those feelings. "I can't help how I feel right now, but I can help how I think and act." Your counselor has materials on feelings.

Extended Activities: Have your students:

1. Journal how they feel on a daily basis.
2. Have books from the library available that handle appropriate expression of feelings.
3. Have some students act out certain feelings to the class. Discuss.
4. Play the game, *Password,* using emotions.

Lesson 25: Showing Your Feeling

1. What do I feel?

2. Why do I feel this way?

3. How can I express what I feel?

4. Choose an appropriate way.

EXPRESSING FEELINGS

Lesson 26: Understanding the Feelings of Others

Objective: Students will identify feelings of others by observing facial expressions and nonverbal body language.

Materials Needed: Photos depicting people expressing various feelings—mad, sad, happy, lonely. Journals.

Establish the Need: How do you know if someone is feeling mad, sad, happy, or lonely? How do you tell with members of your family or friends? I know some people are angry when they stomp off, slam doors, or give me the silent treatment. What are some ways you have learned to tell if people are mad? Sad? Happy? Lonely? List on the board. Make a list of different feelings not already mentioned.

Procedures:

Step 1:   Model the skill:

Model using "Think Aloud" strategies—understanding the feelings of others. Have another adult or a student role play the feelings.

1. Look at the person.
2. Identify the feeling.
3. Choose what I will do.
   A. Comfort.
   B. Inquire.
   C. Ignore.

Step 2:   Role play with feedback:

In groups, have your students look at the photos you have assembled and label the feeling, telling how they decided on that feeling.

Helpful Hints: Teach your students to pay attention to the tone of voice, body language, behavior, and what is said when identifying the feelings of others.

Step 3:   Transfer training

A. **School:** Invite the school counselor to come to class and give a lesson on understanding others' feelings and appropriate responses.

B. **Home/Community:** Journal how your family shows feelings and how they respond to feelings.

C. **Peers:** In small groups have your students label as many feelings as they can think of and identify the characteristics of each.

Comments: There will be many times you can generalize this skill by citing how someone in the news was feeling.

Extended Activities: 1. Write a short story that shows how someone might feel when left out, receiving an award, or having a best friend move.

2. Create a collage with pictures depicting various feelings. Label them.

3. Discuss the feelings in a book or story the class is currently reading. What characteristics does the author use to depict the different feelings?

4. Have your students keep "a feelings journal." Each day, give them a new feeling word to define. Tell if it is a positive or negative emotion, tell of a time he or she experienced it, and illustrate it through drawings or magazine pictures. Doing an ABCs of emotions is a good use of the thesaurus as well as the dictionary.

Expressing Feelings

Lesson 26: Understanding the Feelings of Others

1. Look at the person.

2. Identify the feeling.

3. Choose what I will do.

A. Comfort.

B. Inquire.

C. Ignore.

EXPRESSING FEELINGS

Lesson 27: Knowing What You Are Feeling

Objective: Students will label their own feelings and physical or behavioral characteristics of the feeling.

Materials Needed: "List of Feelings" below, journals.

Establish the Need: Go over each of the feelings on the "List of Feelings" below. Have your students volunteer to depict—by body and facial expression—each feeling. Talk about the physical sensations that can accompany feelings, i.e., tight throat when scared, butterflies in stomach when anxious, fatigue when stressed.

Procedures:

Step 1: **Model the skill:**

Model using "Think Aloud" strategies—knowing what you are feeling.

1. What am I reacting to?
2. What does my body feel?
3. Label the feeling.

Step 2: **Role play with feedback:**

In small groups, have your students role play the feelings from the "List of Feelings."

Step 3: **Transfer training**

A. **School:** You try out for the basketball team and do not make it. How do you feel? Discuss.

B. **Home/Community:** Journal about how you feel about home right now.

C. **Peers:** In small groups, have your students discuss what their physical symptoms are with each feeling.

Comments: It is important for your students to know that feelings are normal and natural. It is our behavioral response to that feeling that we can control.

Extended Activities:

1. Have your students, in groups, write skits depicting someone knowing what he or she is feeling. Put skits on for class.
2. Journal how you know when you are feeling mad, sad, happy, or lonely.
3. Name some physical diseases doctors believe are caused by not knowing our feelings and making appropriate choices for responding to them.
4. Make up a puppet play for another class with the characters getting to know what they are feeling and responding to those feelings.

List of Feelings

Sad, mad, glum, sullen, elated, ecstatic, despondent, furious, repentant, subdued, fearful, anxious, tense, happy, serene, comfortable, jealous, resentful, thoughtful, playful.

Expressing Feelings

Lesson 27: Knowing What
You Are Feeling

1. What am I reacting to?

2. What does my body feel?

3. Label the feeling.

EXPRESSING FEELINGS

Dennis Hanken, Ed.S. and Judith Kennedy, Ed.S.

Lesson 28: Expressing Sympathy

Objective: Students will offer appropriate comments to someone who has experienced a loss.

Materials Needed: Journals.

Establish the Need: Read and discuss.

All her life, Jamie wanted to be a basketball player. She had a hoop in her driveway and she practiced every day she could. Finally, basketball tryouts were scheduled. Jamie was so nervous. She tried to relax and play her best, but so much was at stake! She stepped on her shoelace and fell down; she elbowed another girl when she was trying to block a shot; and she even missed her free throws! She was not picked for the team.

1. How could you express sympathy for Jamie's disappointment?
2. Have you ever had a disappointment similar to Jamie's?

Procedures:

Step 1:   Model the skill:

Model using "Think Aloud" strategies—expressing sympathy for someone's loss.

(1) Has the person experienced a loss or a disappointment? (2) Listen intently to that person. (3) Say, "I'm so sorry...."

Helpful Hints: This is a good time to discuss all the ranges of losses—including death, moving away, being rejected, losing an award, illness, and so forth.

Step 2:   Role play with feedback:

In pairs, have one student tell of an imaginary loss while the other listens and says, "I'm sorry...."

Step 3:   Transfer training

A. **School:** In small groups, ask your students to discuss some disappointments or losses that have occurred at school.

B. **Home/Community:** Journal about a loss or disappointment you have had in your family. Did people express appropriate sympathy?

C. **Peers:** Rejection by peers is a big disappointment for this age. Ask the school counselor to come to class and discuss rejection and some responses.

Comments: If your school has had some tragic loss (suicide or death), have the school psychologist or counselor discuss that and perhaps provide an opportunity to help your students talk about and deal with it.

Extended Activities:

1. Write to a funeral home and get their suggestions for expressing sympathy.
2. Write a letter as a class to someone experiencing a loss.
3. Have a counselor discuss the losses involved in divorce.
4. See "Lesson 60—Grieving."

Lesson 28: Expressing Sympathy

1. Has the person experienced a loss or a disappointment?

2. Listen intently to that person.

3. Say, "I'm so sorry...."

EXPRESSING FEELINGS

Lesson 29: Making Positive Statements

Objective: Students will make positive statements to self and others.

Materials Needed: Journals, drawing paper.

Establish the Need: Read and discuss the following story entitled "Marty and Brad."

Marty and Brad were so different. Marty was always telling people how great he was, how fast he was, and how rich and smart he was. People got so tired of hearing him brag, they would just walk off. But Brad was no easier to be around. He would always say, "I'm dumb, I can't do anything right. No one ever picks me." The other students avoided both Marty and Brad because they got so tired of listening to them.

1. What is the difference between bragging and making positive statements?
2. Why do people put themselves down?

Procedures:

Step 1:   Model the skill:

Model using "Think Aloud" strategies—making positive statements.

1. What can I (or others) do well?
2. State it.

Step 2:   Role play with feedback:

In pairs, have your students take turns naming positive things about themselves, one minute each, and then about the other.

Step 3:   Transfer training

A. **School:** Ask another teacher to make positive statements to the students.

B. **Home/Community:** Assign each student the task of saying one positive statement to each family member this week.

C. **Peers:** Give each student the name of one other student in class with the assignment to write one positive statement about that person.

Comments: For a learning environment to be optimal, students need to hear five positive statements for every one negative.

Extended Activities:

1. Have your students list all their good qualities in their journals.
2. Have them identify one statement they want to be true for themselves, i.e., "I am attractive and intelligent." Write that on a piece of paper, post it somewhere, and read it aloud to themselves five times a day while looking in a mirror.
3. Draw a face of a famous person. Write five to ten positive statements about that person. Did these statements make that person famous?

Lesson 29: Making Positive Statements

1. What can I (or others) do well?

2. State it.

EXPRESSING FEELINGS

Lesson 30: Listening to Other's Problems— What Next?

Objective: Students will demonstrate the skill of listening without taking ownership of another's problem.

Materials Needed: Journals.

Establish the Need: Read and discuss the following story, "Whose Problem Is It?"

Amy was telling Brittany about her parents' marriage problems. April was concerned that her parents would get divorced; they were fighting all the time. Brittany suggested, "Well, why don't you go tell your pastor?" "No," Amy replied, "my parents would be upset if I talked to him." "Well," said Brittany, "how about talking to the counselor at school?" "No, I can't do that, kids would see me," Amy responded. "Well, I guess I could go talk to him for you," Brittany offered.

1. Whose problem is it?
2. Is it a problem Amy can solve?
3. Is it one Brittany can solve?
4. What things could Amy do? Brittany do?

Procedures:

Step 1: Model the skill:

Model using "Think Aloud" strategies—listening without taking ownership.

1. Listen.
2. Whose problem is it?
3. Options—offer suggestions, offer concern.

Step 2: Role play with feedback:

In groups of 3s, have one student talk about a problem, both listen without taking ownership, one offers feedback.

Step 3: Transfer training

A. **School:** Ask other teachers in your core or department to model listening without taking ownership.

B. **Home/Community:** Give the assignment to listen to someone at home without trying to solve that person's problem.

C. **Peers:** Journal about a friend's problem and how you can be supportive.

Comments: If you are a good listener, people might confide in you and want answers. Give them choices, not answers. Otherwise they will blame you for suggestions that don't work.

Extended Activities:

1. Brainstorm with your class ways to be supportive of someone with a problem without taking ownership.

2. All problems aren't solvable, e.g., poverty, global warming, bad marriages, changing peoples' values, and so forth.

Lesson 30: Listening to Other's Problems —What Next?

1. Listen.

2. Whose problem is it?

3. Options.

A. Offer suggestions.

B. Offer concern.

EXPRESSING FEELINGS

Lesson 31: Emotional Rollercoaster— Welcome to Adolescence

Objective: Students will recognize the emotional turbulence of adolescence.

Materials Needed: Journals.

Establish the Need: Read and discuss the following story, "Having a Bad Day."

Mindy couldn't get her hair the way she wanted it. Then her mother yelled at her to get ready to leave. She hadn't even had breakfast. She rushed into school, and Mrs. Morgan yelled at her for being late. Mindy burst into tears and stomped out of class.

1. What do you think was happening with Mindy?

2. How do you deal with the ups and downs of your feelings?

Procedures:

Step 1:　Model the skill:

Model using "Think Aloud" strategies—recognizing emotional ups and downs.

(1) What am I feeling? (2) Does the feeling fit the situation? (3) What can I do to feel better? (4) Should I talk to an adult or a friend for support?

Step 2:　Role play with feedback:

In small groups (it might be better to have boys with boys and girls with girls for this), ask your students to discuss some emotional ups and downs they have experienced this week.

Step 3:　Transfer training

A. **School:** Journal about what makes me feel really good, and really bad, at school

B. **Home/Community:** Write a letter to a family member relating how that person made you feel really good or bad. It may be best not to mail the ones where the feelings are negative. Borrow a paper shredder where students can shred those discreetly.

C. **Peers:** Journal what your friends do to make you feel good or bad. Is there anything you could do so that you feel better more of the time?

Comments: We don't want this to be blaming or making excuses—we are just providing a chance to express some feelings safely. Be sure to stress confidentiality to your students. If they express serious negative feelings, seek counseling assistance.

Extended Activities:

1. Write a paper on what you do to help yourself when you are feeling down.

2. Teach your students to think about, "What's the worst thing that can happen in this situation?" It is often not as bad as they think.

3. Elicit ideas from whole class on ways they can support each other when they feel down. Celebrate when they feel joyous.

Lesson 31: Emotional Rollercoaster— Welcome to Adolescence

1. What am I feeling?

2. Does the feeling fit the situation?

3. What can I do to feel better?

4. Should I talk to an adult or a friend for support?

EXPRESSING FEELINGS

Dennis Hanken, Ed.S. and Judith Kennedy, Ed.S.

Lesson 32: Dealing with Fear

Objective: Students will be able to list the things they fear and then deal with them.

Materials Needed: The dictionary definition: Fear—feeling of alarm of possible danger.

Establish the Need: Eric, a seventh grader, had a speech to give in social studies. The night before he could hardly eat supper and he had trouble falling asleep. The next morning he didn't eat breakfast and went to school with an upset stomach. An hour before class started he was sweating like crazy, even his hands were trembling.

1. What's wrong with Eric?

2. What does Eric need to do so he isn't so upset?

3. Can another student or teacher help Eric?

Read and discuss the story on the next page entitled "Fear of the Dark."

Procedures:

Step 1:   Model the skill:

Establish the scenario that you were invited to go hiking in the hills, but you are afraid of heights. Model using "Think Aloud" strategies—dealing with fear.

1. Identify the reason for my fear.

2. What specific problem caused my fear?

3. Admit—I'm afraid.

4. Choose how to deal with fear.

   A. Breathe slowly.

   B. Think: "What's the worst thing that could happen?"

   C. What am I really worried about? (real or imagined?)

   D. What can I do about it?

   E. Choose and act on it!

Helpful Hints: Being afraid is natural. Most people try to work through their fears. Fears that are very difficult to get over are called *phobias*. Most of the time people worry for no reason, e.g., fear of the dark, fear of heights, or fear of flying. These are real fears, but with the help of adults or friends, you can work them out. People also fear the unknown. You worry you will get hurt, crash or die, but most of the time nothing happens. We need to distinguish between realistic and unrealistic fears.

Step 2:   Role play with feedback:

   A. Talk about fears as a class. Have your students list and then talk about solutions.

   B. Role play a fear you have. Discuss it in small groups.

   C. Have your students distinguish between realistic and unrealistic fears. Role play scenarios.

Relieving Stress

Step 3:   Transfer training

A. **School:** What can cause a fear in school? Discuss, (i.e., getting beat up, failing, being excluded.)

B. **Home/Community:** Discuss a fear you have at home, (i.e., staying alone at night, nightmares.)

C. **Peers:** Boys may be afraid of being beaten up. Girls may fear being made fun of: looks, physique, clothes, and so forth.

Comments: Discuss the difference between worry and fear. Worry is to be anxious or concerned. Fear is a feeling of alarm of possible danger.

Extended Activities: Write down any fears you have—put each one on small piece of paper. Put into basket. Each person draws and tells how he or she would deal with that fear. Use charades to act out "life's most embarrassing moments." The first time this activity is presented, you could write out embarrassing moments you have experienced, e.g., toilet paper stuck to your shoe, walking through the mall or walking out of the restroom with zipper down, trip while walking, missing a step going up or downstairs, and so forth. After the activity, encourage your students to add their ideas and experiences. This reminds students to use humor in difficult situations

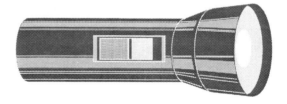

Fear of the Dark

Stacy had a phobia. She wouldn't go out after dark unless she was with someone. She shared her fear with her family and friends. She felt something bad might happen to her, e.g., She might get hurt or someone might be lurking in the shadows. One night, Stacy decided to go first around her house and then around the block without anyone but with a flashlight. Each night she went a little further. Things seemed to be getting better. Soon she didn't need the flashlight. Her self-confidence improved. She still wasn't at ease with the dark; however, she knew it would just take sometime.

1. What was her fear?
2. Was her fear realistic or unrealistic?
3. What was she worried about?
4. What did she do about her fear?
5. Did she conquer the fear forever?
6. How would you handle this situation?

Lesson 32: Dealing with Fear

1. Identify the reason for my fear.

2. What specific problem caused my fear?

3. Admit—I'm afraid.

4. Choose how to deal with fear.

   A. Breathe slowly.

   B. Think: "What's the worst thing that could happen?"

   C. What am I really worried about? (real or imagined?)

   D. What can I do about it?

   E. Choose and act on it!

RELIEVING STRESS

Lesson 33: Dealing with Anxiety

Objective: The student will be able to identify, describe, and then minimize his or her anxiety.

Materials Needed: None.

Establish the Need: Definition of anxiety: Mental uneasiness arising from fear. For example, John disliked competing in band. It wasn't exactly a fear that he had, but he thought he would fail, play the wrong note, and embarrass himself in front of the whole class. Before each competition, he would start to worry, think about failing and contemplate running away. He was his own worst enemy.

1. Was John's anxiety real?

2. Is his reaction normal?

3. What could John do before each competition to make it more tolerable?

Read and discuss the story on the next page, "Will She Ever Smile Again?"

Procedures:

Step 1:   Model the skill:

Model using "Think Aloud" strategies.

1. What caused the anxiety?

2. How am I reacting?

3. What am I thinking about? (List them.)

   A. Are my worries realistic?

   B. Eliminate unrealistic worries.

   C. Change my reaction.

4. See yourself being successful.

Helpful Hints: Everyday is full of challenges, worries, and anxieties. The way to a healthy life is to share with friends and family some of your concerns and do the best you can to meet them head on and conquer them. Although concerns seem overwhelming at times, they are often part of growing up and becoming a more mature person. Talking to a school counselor can also be helpful.

Step 2:   Role play with feedback:

A. Have your students pair up and role play the anxiety they have in their lives. Give feedback. Use "Think Aloud" strategies.

B. Discuss negative thoughts and how that can affect your behavior.

Helpful Hints: Sometimes you think of all the bad things that can happen which also affects how you are going to react. If you can start to feel that some bad things could happen but also good things can happen, then you might start to believe in yourself.

Relieving Stress

Step 3:   Transfer training

A. **School:** Remember one thing that gives you anxiety during the school day. You can lessen your anxiety by talking with someone. Find and practice ways to relax, e.g., breathing, visualization, sense of humor, and so forth.

B. **Home/Community:** There are situations at home that cause anxiety. Discuss.

C. **Peers:** Other students can cause you to have anxiety by teasing or calling you names. Discuss.

Comments: Some people experience more anxiety than others. We are fallible. We can worry so much that it can make us physically sick. It is important to teach your students that stress is normal, but anxiety can be avoided or at least dealt with.

Extended Activities: List some events or situations that create anxiety. Then make a scale (1 to 5) with 1 not a problem and 5 being a bad problem. Then pick one with a 5 and write how you can work through it.

Will She Ever Smile Again?

Dani was mortified when she was told that she had to wear braces on her teeth. None of her friends wore them.

The day she went to the dentist, Dani could hardly eat or sleep, worrying about what everyone would say when they saw her. How could she possibly go to school?

1. What caused the anxiety?
2. How is Dani reacting?
3. What is Dani thinking about? (List.)

    A. Are the fears realistic?

    B. How can Dani eliminate an unrealistic worry?

    C. Can she change her reaction?

Lesson 33: Dealing with Anxiety

1. What caused the anxiety?

2. How am I reacting?

3. What am I thinking about? (List them.)

    A. Are my worries realistic?

    B. Eliminate unrealistic worries.

    C. Change my reaction.

4. See yourself being successful.

RELIEVING STRESS

Lesson 34: Handling Group or Peer Pressure

Objective: Students will recognize peer pressure and choose the appropriate response.

Materials Needed: None.

Establish the Need: Read and discuss:

Rumor has it that Liz is experimenting with drugs. Liz is hanging around students who have access to drugs. Liz gets many stares from questioning classmates. Liz wants to be herself, but she wants to be accepted.

1. Do you think Liz is doing drugs?
2. What choices does she have?

Read and discuss the stories on the next page entitled "The Bad Guy Returns" and "Friendly Persuasion."

Procedures:

Step 1:   Model the skill:

Model using "Think Aloud" strategies—Use the scenario that friends want you to steal some candy from a store just for the thrill of it.

1. What do they want me to do?
2. Should I do it?
3. Make a choice:

    A. Say, "No."

    B. Delay your answer—it may eventually be dropped.

    C. Avoid the person making the request.

    D. Say, "I don't think that's a good idea."

4. Stick to your decision.

Gender Differences: Boys often put pressure on other boys to do something daring or sneaky. Girls may put pressure on each other about dress, makeup, going out with boys, or something that draws attention to self, (i.e., tattoos, body piercing). It takes a strong will to say "no" and not to conform.

Step 2:   Role play with feedback:

A. In groups of three, have your students practice handling peer pressure. One student pressures, one practices refusal skills, and the other observes and gives feedback. Rotate the roles.

B. Role play positive peer pressure, i.e., running for student council, joining a team. Discuss.

Step 3:   Transfer training

A. **School:** A new student wants to copy your math assignment. What should you say? Your best friend wants to copy your assignment. What do you say?

B. **Home/Community:** A new friend wants you to go window peeking just for the thrill of it. What should you say?

C. **Peers:** One of your classmates likes you, but is really a bully to all the rest of the class. What should you do?

Comments: Peer pressure follows you through life. You can't be liked by everyone. Would a true friend ask you to do something wrong or get you in trouble?

Extended Activities: Discuss the peer pressure you are under as you get older.

What pressure do you feel when you:

1. Date?

2. Go to parties?

3. Go out after dark with other students?

4. Go to someone's house for a weekend?

5. Borrow expensive things from friends?

The Bad Guy Returns

Jerry, an eighth grade student, just spent some time in a juvenile correction center for trying to steal a car. He comes back to school and acts like he has changed. However, he starts to threaten other students. He wants their lunch money.

Should you:

A. Tell a teacher or principal?

B. Tell your parents?

C. Ignore the situation?

D. Get a bunch of boys to beat him up?

Friendly Persuasion

You are on an island. There are three of you. Wango, Tango, and Bongo. Bongo has an idea. We are stranded here with no chance of rescue. Wango and Tango agree, but what can we do? Bongo says, "Let's build a raft and take our chances on the open sea." Wango and Tango can't swim. The question is: Will Wango and Tango join Bongo on the sea or will Bongo build the boat and try it himself?

How can one person persuade others?

Can two exert more pressure to change opinions than one?

Lesson 34: Handling Group or Peer Pressure

1. What do they want me to do?

2. Should I do it?

3. Make a choice:

   A. Say, "No."

   B. Delay your answer—it may eventually be dropped.

   C. Avoid the person making the request.

   D. Say, "I don't think that's a good idea."

4. Stick to your decision.

RELIEVING STRESS

Lesson 35: Stating a Complaint

Objective: Students will be able to state a complaint to adults or peers.

Materials Needed: None.

Establish the Need: John lent Ben his favorite CD for the weekend. Ben gave it back to him on Monday. When John went to play his CD, there were deep scratches that disrupted the play. John was really upset.

1. What should John say to Ben?

2. How could he state the complaint without hurting the friendship?

Read and discuss the stories, "Stating a Complaint to a Teacher" and "I Deserve It," on the next page.

Procedures:

Step 1:	Model the skill:

Model using "Think Aloud" strategies—stating a complaint.

1. What injustice have I suffered?

2. Decide when and to whom to complain.

3. Use a firm voice and be polite, "Excuse me, I have a problem."

4. Keep trying to resolve the issue.

Helpful Hints: Sometimes you just accept bad things that happen to you. However, there are times when you have to speak up to protect yourself and your property.

Step 2:	Role play with feedback:

A. Group your students into groups of three or four and pick a situation, e.g., bought a new shirt or dress and it doesn't fit. You have to bring it back. Have each student practice stating the complaint. Rotate and discuss.

B. Role play making a complaint to an adult or teacher. Teach them that unfair rules exist in school and society.

Step 3:	Transfer training

A. **School:** Practice stating complaints with the principal in an appropriate way.

B. **Home/Community:** Practice stating a complaint to your parents about something that seems unfair, e.g., curfew, chores.

C. **Peers:** Practice a complaint to a fellow student who is annoying or bothersome.

Comments: Everybody has the right to state a complaint about a legitimate wrong issue. What is the difference between a complaint, whining, or being negative?

Extended Activities: Have your students attend a school board meeting or a city (town) council meeting to see how the members deal with complaints.

    1. What about accusing somebody by mistake?

    2. How would you feel?

    3. How would you make amends?

Stating a Complaint to a Teacher

John took an essay test in social studies. The teacher gave him very little points for one of his answers. Therefore, his grade was a C- instead of the B- he had hoped for. John was upset about the grade and question so he asked his friends and parents about his answer and what they thought. They all agreed that he didn't receive enough points for his answer. The next day John went to the teacher and politely asked if he would consider his question. The teacher agreed to read the answer. He also agreed that John should receive some additional points, but not quite as many as John thought he should receive. But, John was also pleased with himself. He did a good job of presenting the issue to his teacher without whining and complaining, doing it in a respectful, sincere, and meaningful way.

I Deserve It

Pretend you have a job and you want a raise. You feel unappreciated because you work hard.

What should be your demeanor or looks and tone of voice when you ask for a raise?

Relieving Stress

Lesson 35: Stating a Complaint

1. What injustice have I suffered?

2. Decide when and to whom to complain.

3. Use a firm voice and be polite, "Excuse me, I have a problem."

4. Keep trying to resolve the issue.

RELIEVING STRESS

Lesson 36: Responding to a Complaint

Objective: Students will listen to a complaint about self and respond politely.

Materials Needed: Here is a list of places: Sears, McDonalds, church, school, and home. Do you know who handles the complaints in each of these places?

Establish the Need: Nicky was the president of the eighth grade class. As the year went on, more and more students complained to her about certain problems at school. She didn't have any control over some of these problems. Just because you are a class officer, it doesn't mean you need to hear all the complaints about school.

     1. Should Nicky refer these students to the principal?

     2. Was Nicky being taken advantage of by the students?

Procedures:

Step 1: Model the skill:

Model using "Think Aloud" strategies.

     1. Listen to the complaint.

     2. Think before responding.

     3. Ask questions, if necessary.

     4. Choose a response:

         A. Apologize.

         B. Compromise.

         C. Do nothing.

         D. Deny any wrong doing.

Helpful Hints: Some students and adults become defensive when hearing a complaint. Other reactions could be: argumentative, show anger, accuse others, denial, and so forth.

Step 2: Role play with feedback:

     A. In groups of three or four students, role play answering a complaint, e.g., cheating in a game, breaking a friend's CD, dropping or breaking a soda in the store, being accused of cheating or lying.

     B. Answer a complaint by a teacher for a late assignment or poor grade.

Helpful Hints: Your tone of voice is very important when responding to a complaint.

Relieving Stress

Step 3:   Transfer training

A. **School:** The principal is upset with your class because of some inappropriate behavior during a fire drill. How does the class handle the complaint?

B. **Home/Community:** Your father is mad at you because you have a D in one of your core classes. How do you handle it?

C. **Peers:** Your best friend had a complaint about you and it wasn't true. How do you handle that situation?

Comments: Responding to a complaint can be difficult. Being falsely accused can have the same impact as being rightly accused. Talk about some movie stars or government officials being accused in the newspapers. What sometimes happens to them if they are innocent? If guilty?

Extended Activities: What happens to people if they are wrongly accused, but still end up in jail?

Have your students think of a famous person who may have been wrongly accused.

1. How did that change that person's life?

2. What about someone in your town?

3. Have you ever been wrongly accused?

4. Have you ever wrongly accused someone?

How do you think a judge in a court handles listening to complaints all day?

Is it more difficult to respond to a complaint if you know that person? Your friends? Parents? Teachers?

Pretend you are wrongly accused of stealing something. Ask for volunteers. Act this out to the class. Discuss.

Lesson 36: Responding to a Complaint

1. Listen to the complaint.

2. Think before responding.

3. Ask questions, if necessary.

4. Choose a response:

   A. Apologize.

   B. Compromise.

   C. Do nothing.

   D. Deny any wrong doing.

RELIEVING STRESS

Lesson 37: Sportsmanship

Objective: Students will learn how to win and lose appropriately.

Materials Needed: None.

Establish the Need: Bob and John always play football on the same team. This year they are both eighth graders. Every time they lost a game, they would curse, lose their temper, and not talk to anybody. After he had given them several warnings, the coach decided to kick them off the team.

1. Did the coach do the right thing?
2. Should he have given them another chance?
3. Could Bob and John have done anything differently?

Procedures:

Step 1: **Model the skill:**

Model using "Think Aloud" strategies—showing good sportsmanship.

1. Follow the rules of the game.
2. Be courteous to the other team.
3. Give encouragement to other players.
4. After the game, congratulate the other team by shaking hands or saying "good game."

Step 2: **Role play with feedback:**

A. In small groups, have your students role play losing a game using "Think Aloud" strategies.

B. In small groups, have your students role play winning a game using "Think Aloud" strategies.

Step 3: **Transfer training**

A. **School:** Observe how your school's team reacts after winning and losing. Discuss.

B. **Home/Community:** Discuss how your family reacts to winning and losing.

C. **Peers:** Discuss how your friends react to losing. Do "poor sports" encourage each other? Do "good sports" influence others?

Comments: Your students will have seen many examples of poor sportsmanship on TV and everyday life. Discuss some examples.

Extended Activities: Has pro sports added to the problem of sportsmanship in our schools? Ask your students to discuss what sports mean to them? (Winning, losing, or just having fun?) Have them write a brief play—just a scene or two—depicting good sportsmanship vs. poor sportsmanship. Pick any sport, perhaps a variety of sports, and then video tape the results. This could be done in groups and then have all groups give each other feedback after watching the videos.

Play a game in class just for fun, i.e., spelling contest. Now change it so it is the boys against the girls. How does competition change the flavor?

Have your students talk about sportsmanship in Little League, high school, college, pro sports. What are the differences?

Discuss fan sportsmanship.

Discuss the behavior of parents, coaches, and fellow players.

Lesson 37: Sportsmanship

1. Follow the rules of the game.

2. Be courteous to the other team.

3. Give encouragement to other players.

4. After the game, congratulate the other team by shaking hands or saying "good game."

RELIEVING STRESS

Lesson 38: Defending a Friend

Objective: Students will defend a friend who is being treated unfairly.

Materials Needed: None.

Establish the Need: Nicole and Sarah were best of friends. Nicole was being teased by several other girls. Sarah decided she had heard and seen enough. She told the other girls that if they didn't back off, she would talk to the principal or talk to their parents.

    1. Did Sarah have the right to defend her friend?

    2. Should Nicole say something to the girls or was she intimidated?

Read and discuss the story entitled "Best Friend" on the next page.

Procedures:

Step 1:   **Model the skill:**

Model using "Think Aloud" strategies—

    1. Decide if a friend is being treated unfairly.

    2. Decide if a friend needs my help.

    3. How can I help my friend?

        A. Tell an adult.

        B. Speak up.

    4. Make the right choice.

Step 2:   **Role play with feedback:**

    A. In groups of three, have your students role play with each taking turns defending a friend. Scenario—Your friend is wrongly accused of taking someone's watch.

    B. Have them defend a friend to a teacher or adult.

Step 3:   **Transfer training**

    A. **School:** Ask your students to practice this skill at lunch, in the hallway, or on the bus.

    B. **Home/Community:** Have you defended a family member in the last six months? Discuss.

    C. **Peers:** Report the last time you defended a friend. Would you do it again?

Comments: Standing up for another person takes courage. Discuss.

Extended Activities: Should you lie to defend a friend? Make a list of famous people who stood up for others, i.e., Martin Luther King, Ghandi, Clarence Darrow, Harriet Tubman. Do lawyers defend for money or friendship? Pretend you are a lawyer defending a friend. Have a mock trial. There is no stronger alliance than true friendship. Define friendship. Sometimes friends need all the support they can get, especially during difficult times, e.g., a death in the family, divorce, or moving.

Relieving Stress

Best Friend

John and Mike were the best of buds. Mike got in trouble for cheating on a test. He had the same wrong answers as John; but it turns out they had studied together from the same incorrect notes. Mike had not copied from John's paper. John knew what had happened and decided to intervene on Mike's behalf with the teacher.

1. Should John go to the teacher for Mike and try to help?
2. Should John let Mike do this himself?
3. Did Mike really cheat?
4. What is cheating?

Dennis Hanken, Ed.S. and Judith Kennedy, Ed.S.

Lesson 38: Defending a Friend

1. Decide if a friend is being treated unfairly.

2. Decide if a friend wants my help.

3. How can I help my friend?

A. Tell an adult.

B. Speak up.

4. Make the right choice.

RELIEVING STRESS

Lesson 39: Being Left Out

Objective: Students will be able to handle the feeling of being left out.

Materials Needed: None.

Establish the Need: Several of the eighth graders were planning a big Valentine's Day party. The party included the most popular students. Many other students were left out, even though it was supposed to be for the entire class.

1. How do you think the students who were left out felt?

2. Why do some students exclude others?

Read and discuss the story on the next page entitled "Just Keep Trying."

Procedures:

Step 1:   Model the skill:

Model using "Think Aloud" strategies—

1. Why am I feeling left out?

2. What can I do about it?

   A. Ask to join.

   B. Tell how I feel to an adult or friend.

   C. Find something else to do.

3. Make decisions.

Gender Differences: This might be more of an issue for girls in adolescence. However, all people can identify with having been left out.

Step 2:   Role play with feedback:

A. In groups of two using "Think Aloud" strategies, discuss experiences of being left out. Rotate and discuss. Imaginary scenarios may be best.

B. Discuss how being left out can be a blessing or a positive situation.

Step 3:   Transfer training

A. **School:** Discuss being left out of class participation or being left off the school team.

B. **Home/Community:** Discuss being left out of a neighborhood game because you're too small.

C. **Peers:** Discuss the times you have been left out of a game or birthday party. What were your feelings?

Comments: Being left out can affect a person's self-confidence.

Extended Activities: Throughout history there have been occasions when people were left out. Can you add to this list? Astronauts who didn't get to go to the moon, presidential candidates who lost an election, people who were passed over on job promotions, people who didn't fit in at school or job, and so forth.

Just Keep Trying

Ellie was a very active and fairly popular seventh grade girl. However, she wasn't very athletic and she had crooked teeth. Because of this she was often left out of games in PE and some parties. She was getting very discouraged. Then, last summer, she began to run and work out at the YMCA. She became stronger and practiced with other girls in volleyball and basketball. She was definitely making an attempt to change and not to be left out. Then she decided to ask her parents if she could get braces. Her parents didn't have dental insurance. She said she would mow lawns in the summer and baby-sit as much as she could to pay for half the cost. Her parents agreed. After all this, she was much more accepted in school. She made an effort to change.

1. Did Ellie answer the question, "Why was she left out?"
2. Did she do something about it?
3. Should her parents have tried to fix her teeth before she was teased?
4. Is it always a good idea to change yourself to fit in?
5. Is it more important to be true to yourself or change to fit in?
6. Were the changes for her or purely to fit in?

Relieving Stress

Lesson 39: Being Left Out

1. Why am I feeling left out?

2. What can I do about it?

A. Ask to join.

B. Tell how I feel to an adult or friend.

C. Find something else to do.

3. Make decisions.

RELIEVING STRESS

Dennis Hanken, Ed.S. and Judith Kennedy, Ed.S.

Getting to Know You!

Lesson 40: Responding to Failure

Objective: Students will learn to handle failure in a positive way.

Materials Needed: None.

Establish the Need: Do we learn by failure? There are several times in a lifetime that our failures can change our goals and even our future.

Gus was a "C" student who loved to play football. He studied hard and realized that if he wanted to play football, he would have to maintain a "C" average—school policy. For the first nine weeks of the eighth grade, Gus was failing pre-algebra. He was afraid of being dropped from football.

1. What should Gus do?

2. Should Gus quit football and study more?

3. Because Gus is such a good football player, should the school make an exception for him?

Read and discuss the story, "If At First you Don't Succeed, Try Again," on the next page.

Procedures:

Step 1:   Model the skill:

Model using "Think Aloud" strategies—failing a test in school.

1. Why did I fail?

2. What do I do now?

   A. Try again.

   B. Do something else.

   C. Ask for help.

3. What can I do to prevent failing next time?

Helpful Hints: If we give up when we fail, that usually doesn't accomplish anything. Anybody can quit—everybody fails sometime during a lifetime. But, the ones who keep trying usually succeed. If you give up, you will never know success. Failure is learning; quitting is losing.

Step 2:   Role play with feedback:

A. In small groups, each person brings up a failure, then using "Think Aloud" strategies, answer the question, "Did you respond to failure in a positive way?"

B. Discuss a failure in your life when you didn't respond in a positive way. When you gave up!

Helpful Hints: There are many things you fail at, but how you respond is the true test. Examples: failing a test, didn't make the school team, didn't make first chair, received the lowest score on a test, can't speak in front of groups, and so forth.

Educational Media Corporation®, Box 21311, Minneapolis, MN 55421-0311   117

Step 3:   Transfer training

    A. **School:** Ask your students how many ever failed a test? How did they respond afterwards? Study harder or give up?

    B. **Home/Community:** Ask parents if they ever failed at something? What happened?

    C. **Peers:** When your best friend fails at something, do you offer support?

Comments: When people fail, does it involve chance, luck, or motivation? What is failure?

Failure can happen once or many times. Failing a test versus going to jail. Not trying is failure. Excuses are attempts to explain failure.

Extended Activities:

1. Share "Tips for Doing Well on a Test'" on the next page.

2. How can you avoid failure? Try your best?

3. Is a person a failure because he or she fails once in awhile? What about bums, homeless people, or criminals?

If At First You Don't Succeed, Try Again"

Eric failed seventh grade Math. He knew he failed because he didn't try very hard. With his parents, he decided to go to summer school to improve his skills. He didn't want to ruin his summer, but he deserved the consequence. He passed summer school. In eighth grade math, he tried harder and passed the course. And yes, he had the best summer that year, because he didn't have to go to summer school.

1. Is going to summer school a natural consequence for Eric?

2. Did he respond to the consequence?

3. Eric made a good choice. What could have been a bad choice for him?

Tips for Doing Well on a Test

1. Go to bed on time the night before and get up in time for a good breakfast.

2. Be sure you have all the materials you need—a sharpened pencil, paper, books, notes, maps, whatever you need.

3. Read the directions before starting the test. If you don't understand something, ask your teacher.

4. Answer all the questions you know first, leaving the ones you are uncertain of until later. However, it is usually best not to go back and change your answers, as your first response is often correct.

5. Be sure that you answer every question.

6. Stay relaxed. If your mind wanders or you feel anxious, breathe deeply.

7. Check the clock periodically to make sure you will have enough time to complete the test. Don't hurry. Use the time you need.

8. Check your finished paper before handing it in to make sure you answered every item..

9. Study a little each day prior to the test, instead of waiting until the last minute.

Lesson 40: Responding to Failure

1. Why did I fail?

2. What do I do now?

A. Try again.

B. Do something else.

C. Ask for help.

3. What can I do to prevent failing next time?

RELIEVING STRESS

Lesson 41: Handling Threats

Objective: Students will be able to handle threats in a calm manner and respond accordingly.

Materials Needed: None.

Establish the Need: Being threatened by a peer or an adult is a very serious problem. It can happen to anyone. Rumors and gossip are one type of threat and can cause disastrous conflicts. People can threaten students outside and inside school. Students can be forced to do things they shouldn't or can be put in situations to be beaten up or threatened. Share with your students a time you were threatened and what you did. Discuss examples from history or current news. Elicit examples of threats from your students and ways the threats were handled.

Read and discuss the story, "Protecting a Buddy," on the next page.

Procedures:

Step 1: Model the skill:

Model using "Think Aloud" strategies.

1. Is the threat serious or dangerous?
2. What are my options?
   A. Tell friends.
   B. Tell an adult.
   C. Report it to the police or a liaison officer.
3. Take action to stay safe.

Helpful Hints: Don't be secretive about this. Discuss threats with someone you trust.

Step 2: Role play with feedback:

A. Role play an incident where you are being threatened by another student and that a person is going to beat you up. What would you do? Use "Think Aloud" strategies. Discuss.

B. Ask others if this has ever happened to them. Discuss. Find articles in the newspaper or magazines that address this issue. Discuss. What did the person do? What were the results?

Helpful Hints: Discuss stalking. Can stalking occur in school?

Step 3: Transfer training

A. **School:** Discuss threats at school activities, fights at games, date rape. Ask your school counselor to talk to your students.

B. **Home/Community:** Parents can threaten students. Discuss physical abuse, emotional abuse, and verbal abuse.

C. **Peers:** What should you do if you are followed by a stranger? Discuss.

Comments: Our society can't always protect us 24 hours a day. How do we protect ourselves against threats if police aren't available? Ideas: Lock your car and house, don't travel alone, tell someone you trust to help, avoid dangerous situations.

Extended Activities: Make a list of ways that people threaten others, i.e., someone threatens to shoot someone, someone hurts another person, someone threatens to rape or intimidate a person.

1. Why do some celebrities seem to get more threats?
2. Why is it necessary to have body guards to protect high-profile people?
3. Brainstorm and list all the ways we can keep ourselves safe.
4. List ways students and staff can make your school a safer place. Your town. Your country.

Protecting a Buddy

John was a typical eighth grader. One day in gym he got into a shouting match with a gang member. That gang member threatened John with bodily harm after school. The gym teacher did not hear the threat. John went to talk to the principal. The principal talked to the gang member. The principal had John's parents pick him up after school for the next two weeks. The gang member was placed in another class. This seemed to work, but John was still scared for many weeks to come. John's friends also protected him whenever possible. This gang member was eventually arrested for threatening others in school, thanks to John and others.

1. What did John do that was a good response to the treat?
2. What other things might he have done?

Dennis Hanken, Ed.S. and Judith Kennedy, Ed.S.

Lesson 41: Handling Threats

1. Is the threat serious or dangerous?

2. What are my options?

A. Tell friends.

B. Tell an adult.

C. Report it to the police or a liaison officer.

3. Take action to stay safe.

RELIEVING STRESS

Lesson 42: How to Relax and Deal with Stress

Objective: Students will be able to recognize stress and learn to relax.

Materials Needed: None.

Establish the Need: Everyone experiences stress in their lives at one time or other. Sometimes the stress comes from within, (i.e., determination, worry, fear, or self-motivation) and sometimes it comes from outside forces. Either way can be bothersome. Sometimes we get so uptight that we displace our frustration on someone close to us. Some stress is good because it can motivate us to do better. Too much stress is harmful and can cause physical symptoms of distress, (i.e., stomachache, headache, nausea, fatigue, nervousness). These can lead to more serious problems if the stress is long-term. Relaxing or using positive self-talk can help us maintain a balance when dealing with stress. All of us have ways to relax. In adolescence, we are in search of our own way to relax. Exercise, laughter, prayer, taking with someone we trust, meditation, and a change in routine are all ways to handle stress.

Name other ways to handle stress. Read and discuss the story on the next page entitled "Organize and Prioritize."

Procedures:

Step 1:   Model the skill:

Model using "Think Aloud" strategies—preparing for a test.

1. What is causing my stress?
2. Am I overreacting?
3. What are my options?
   A. Talk to someone.
   B. Exercise.
   C. Deal with the problem.
4. Make a choice.

Gender Differences: Boys may handle stress differently than girls. Boys may get more angry, throw things, fight, curse, be aggressive. Girls might quit eating or eat more, or withdraw or sleep more, although they can exhibit anger too.

Step 2:   Role play with feedback:

A. Discuss sources of stress in school and at home. Role play handling a stressful situation.

B. Now role play how you would handle it differently, using some of the strategies listed.

Helpful Hints: Stress may be caused by worrying over trivial matters and not remembering the positive side to all situations, i.e., if you failed a course, you can take it again. If you lose a boyfriend or girlfriend, you can find another. If you tear a hole in a new shirt, you can have it fixed or buy a new one. Optimism versus pessimism. A positive outlook is better than a negative outlook. Stress is sometimes caused by procrastinating. Discuss examples of this with your students. What is the solution to this?

Step 3:   Transfer training

A. **School:** When you feel stress at school, talk to your teachers or school counselor.

B. **Home/Community:** When stress occurs at home, can you be honest with your parents and discuss it openly?

C. **Peers:** When stress occurs from negative peer pressure, be honest, say this is wrong, and deal with it.

Comments: Stress happens at all ages. Many times it is self-inflicted. Stress can bring on a variety of physical ailments if it is not dealt with. We may worry too much. Stress cannot be avoided altogether. It is important that your students learn to handle stressful situations.

Extended Activities: Make a list of the stress that you experienced during the past year. How did you handle the pressure? How can you make changes in the way you react? Asking for help from peers and adults can help you make a plan of action for problems. Stress usually appears when you have a problem that can't be easily solved, or when situations occur simultaneously, like homework or tests.

Organize and Prioritize

John, an eighth grader, had tons of homework one week along with several tests. He was a mess. He couldn't eat or sleep very well just thinking about it. He couldn't even figure out where to start. Finally, he asked his mother to help him. She suggested that he organize his time, prioritize his subjects, and ask for help at school. He agreed and finally got some relief. He didn't do everything perfect, but at least he had a plan and could think logically. He was much less stressed.

1. What are some ways you bring stress into your life?
2. What are some things you could do differently to decrease stress?

Lesson 42: How to Relax and Deal with Stress

1. What is causing my stress?

2. Am I overreacting?

3. What are my options?

A. Talk to someone.

B. Exercise.

C. Deal with the problem.

4. Make a choice.

RELIEVING STRESS

Lesson 43: Dealing with Physical Changes

Objective: Students will identify physical changes and ways to deal with them.

Materials Needed: None.

Establish the Need: As we develop in adolescence, there are many physical changes. With these changes come feelings and drives that are new and different. Girls may end up crying more. They may be more conscious of their looks. Boys don't usually grow as fast as girls in early adolescence; they grow in spurts. Adolescents are trying to find their place. This is a time where you are not a child, but not fully an adult either.

Give some examples to your students of how physical changes can create discomfort.

Read and discuss the stories on the next page, "Changes—For the Good" and "A Do Over."

Procedures:

Step 1: Model the skill:

Model using "Think Aloud" strategies.

1. How am I changing?
2. How do I feel about the change?
3. Change is part of adolescence.

Gender Differences: Boys tend to have greater differences of size and can be teased about it. Unusually big girls may get teased. Being pretty or cute is very important to girls at this age.

Step 2: Role play with feedback:

A. Small groups of 3s. Discuss physical changes in adolescence. Role play issues involving height or large shoe size. Avoid talking about weight.

B. Role play about different people in the world who are unique, i.e., people who are 7' tall, people who are beautiful or ugly. How do they cope? Why do we label people?

Helpful Hints: This is a very "touchy" subject. So if kids don't want to say much, be accepting. Should you like a person only because of looks?

Step 3: Transfer training

A. **School:** If you are concerned about size or weight, you can talk to a school counselor about the issue. Diet and genetics play a big role.

B. **Home/Community:** If you are concerned about weight or size, ask your parents about relatives on both sides. Consult your doctor if it is a real big issue; your doctor might be able to help.

C. **Peers:** A friend who is too small to play baseball might be great at soccer. Suggest other options. Try to see the positive qualities for peers who are perceived as too small, too heavy, or too tall.

Comments: Everybody wants to look great and be just the right weight and height.

It is important to accept the way you are. You may want to change something you can change. There's not much that can be done about height. Diet can change weight to a degree. Haircuts and makeup can enhance. Some authorities believe telling a person he or she is too heavy or too skinny can lead to eating disorders.

Extended Activities: Have the nurse discuss the wide range of height and weight for adolescence. Discuss different ways to change your looks. Discuss the importance of accepting how we look. Have the nurse discuss eating disorders and the emphasis in our society on females being thin.

Changes—For the Good

Bob was kind of a small sixth grade boy with red hair and a freckled face. He was teased a lot. However, by the time he was in the 8th grade, he had broad shoulders and was the tallest in his class. The freckles made him even cuter. The girls loved his red hair.

What a difference two years made to Bob!

1. How do you think Bob handled all the changes?
2. How do you think Bob saw himself before, during, and after the changes?

A Do Over

Jill was a plain seventh grade girl who didn't like the way she looked. She loved to baby sit and she had some extra money. Her mother suggested she go to the beauty salon to get her hair changed. She got her hair dyed and cut, a little eye shadow, and some cute modern clothes. The other kids loved her new look and she was the talk of all the boys in the seventh grade.

1. What would you have done if you were Jill?
2. Do looks mean everything to us? Should they?
3. What could Jill change that would also make her life better?

Relieving Stress

Lesson 43: Expressing Physical Changes

1. How am I changing?

2. How do I feel about the change?

3. Change is part of adolescence.

RELIEVING STRESS

Lesson 44: Whose Problem Is It?

Objective: Student will decide the ownership of a problem and take responsibility if theirs.

Materials Needed: None.

Establish the Need: Read and discuss the following story entitled "The Foul Ball."

Kip and Tom were playing baseball in the vacant lot on their street. It was Tom's turn at bat. He hit a foul ball which went through the Bentley's window. "Oh, no, look what you did!" yelled Kip. Tom said, "It wasn't my fault. It was your fault. You pitched the ball all wrong." "I did not," yelled Kip. They were still arguing when Mr. Bentley walked up.

1. Whose problem is it?
2. What are some possible solutions?

Procedures:

Step 1:	Model the skill:

Model using "Think Aloud" strategies—deciding ownership of problem.

1. Whose problem is it?
2. Is it mine?
3. If so, what can I do to solve it? What are my choices? Pick the best one.

Step 2:	Role play with feedback:

A. Brainstorm ideas for problems to be role played such as: loss of a borrowed items, theft, parent problems, friendship problems, poor grades, and being late for something.

B. In groups, role play being accused of something; decide on ownership and solutions.

Step 3:	Transfer training

A. **School:** You are accused of cheating on a test. What do you do?

B. **Home/Community:** You oversleep and you don't have time for breakfast before the bus. Whose problem is it?

C. **Peers:** You and Mike are friends. Mike is angry that he didn't get picked for the soccer team. He yells at you. Is it your problem?

Comments: It is extremely difficult for some people to accept responsibility. Some students may need guidance in this.

Extended Activities:

1. Develop a list of scenarios and have your students decide whose problem each is and list solutions.
2. Discuss current events. Describe a problem, ownership, and solutions.
3. Identify a problem in the local community, ownership, and solutions.
4. Explain to your students that with complaints they should also be able to formulate a plan of action to solve the problem.

Lesson 44: Whose Problem Is It?

1. Whose problem is it?

2. Is it mine?

3. If so, what can I do to solve it? What are my choices? Pick the best one.

MAKING DECISIONS

Lesson 45: Making Good or Bad Decisions

Objective: Students will identify decisions, the consequences of each, and judge whether a decision was good or bad.

Materials Needed: Clippings of articles from newspapers and magazines involving decisions that have been made, e.g., for the schools, city, parks, and so forth.

Establish the Need: Read each clipping you have gathered and have the students decide if the decision made was good or bad and what the consequence of each is or may be.

Procedures:

Step 1: Model the skill:

Model using "Think Aloud" strategies—deciding if a decision is good or bad by its consequences.

1. What is the situation?
2. Name three possible decisions.
3. Name the consequences of each.
4. Act on the best choice.

Step 2: Role play with feedback:

Group your students in threes or fours. Give the scenario: The group of kids you hang out with are going to the mall tonight. You want to go, but your mom wants you to watch your little brother. Also, you have a unit science test tomorrow.

1. Name three decisions and the consequences of each.
2. Have your students record and share with class.

Step 3: Transfer training

A. **School:** You want to go watch the debate tournament, but you're not done with your algebra assignment. List decisions and consequences.

B. **Home/Community:** You know your parent has to work late tonight. You decide to fix dinner. What might the consequences be?

C. **Peers:** A group of kids are going out over lunch and drink beer in their cars; they invite you. What are some decisions and consequences?

Comments: Evaluating the consequence of a decision is good practice. You will find many opportunities to reinforce this.

Extended Activities:

1. Brainstorm scenarios in groups and present them to the class with the decisions and consequences of each.
2. Use the decision-making model for class decisions.
3. In the stories you read for language arts, discuss the decisions the characters made and other possible decisions and consequences.

Dennis Hanken, Ed.S. and Judith Kennedy, Ed.S.

Lesson 45: Making Good or Bad Decisions

1. What is the situation?

2. Name three possible decisions.

3. Name the consequences of each.

4. Act on the best choice.

MAKING DECISIONS

Lesson 46: Applying My Abilities in a Positive Way

Objective: Students will identify their abilities and ways to apply each one toward a positive goal.

Materials Needed: None.

Establish the Need: Read and discuss the following story entitled "Summer."

Brian and Amanda were talking after school about what they wanted to do this summer. Brian said, "I'm going to check into working for a veterinarian, because I think I might want to be a vet when I grow up. This would give me some first hand experience." "Are you kidding?" scoffed Amanda. "I'm going to tan on the beach, water ski, shop at the mall, and catch the newest movies in town." "But you are so good at teaching children," said Brian. "I thought you were going to teach swimming lessons." "Not me! Life is too short, and I want to play," said Amanda.

1. What are the positive qualities of each person?

2. How are they applying these qualities in a positive way?

Procedures:

Step 1:　Model the skill:

Model using "Think Aloud" strategies—identifying abilities and applying them in a positive way.

1. What am I good at?

2. How do I want to use that ability?

3. Am I applying it in a positive way?

Step 2:　Role play with feedback:

A. In their journals, have your students list five abilities. Identify how each of those abilities might be applied toward a positive goal.

B. In pairs, have your students share and give ideas to each other.

Helpful Hints: Be sure to emphasize that the students are to help each other find positive attributes of themselves and each other. Then they may creatively brainstorm ways to apply those attributes toward a goal.

Step 3:　Transfer training

A. **School:** Ask other teachers in your core or grade level to be prepared to assist students with identifying attributes and ways to apply them.

B. **Home/Community:** Have each student ask a family member to name one positive quality about the student.

C. **Peers:** As a class, discuss some of the qualities needed to be a coach, doctor, mechanic, computer programmer, teacher, and so forth.

Comments: Some students may have trouble naming their attributes. This is good practice.

Extended Activities:

1. Have your students take a vocational interest inventory, such as the *Strong Campbell*. The school counselor or psychologist is a good resource for this.

2. Arrange for community people representing various vocations to come and talk to your class about qualities needed for that profession and some ways to work toward entering that profession.

3. Are students at this age realistic about their future? Is wishing okay?

4. Is wanting to play in the NFL or NBA realistic? Or to be an actress? Should you have high or low expectations? Most people want high glamour jobs. Can everyone have a high profile job?

Making Decisions

Lesson 46: Applying My Abilities in a Positive Way

1. What am I good at?

2. How do I want to use that ability?

3. Am I applying it in a positive way?

MAKING DECISIONS

Dennis Hanken, Ed.S. and Judith Kennedy, Ed.S.

Lesson 47: Gathering Information

Objective: Student will list sources of information.

Materials Needed: Access to library and Internet.

Establish the Need: Read and discuss the following story entitled "Finding Information."

Brad wanted to be involved in the space program when he grew up, but he didn't have any idea what kind of training was needed or where the training was offered. He didn't even know what courses he should take in school to prepare. He went to see Mr. Anderson, school counselor, for some ideas. "Well, Brad, I really don't know either, but how could we find out?" asked Mr. Anderson.

List some sources where Brad could find:

  A. Prerequisite courses for a profession?

  B. What universities offered these programs?

  C. What the university program would entail?

Procedures:

Step 1:   **Model the skill:**

Model using "Think Aloud" strategies—finding information about something that interests you.

  1. What information do I need?

  2. Where can I find the information?

    A. Library.

    B. Internet.

    C. People.

    D. Agencies.

Step 2:   **Role play with feedback:**

  A. Assign your students something to look up and report on. You may want to have them work in pairs or small groups.

  B. Brainstorm with your class all the sources of information they can think of.

Step 3:   **Transfer training**

  A. **School:** Have your students find a college which offers the program they want to follow.

  B. **Home/Community:** Who in your family or neighborhood is a good source of information?

  C. **Peers:** With another student, decide on a vocation and find information about it.

Comments: We are in the information age. Brainstorm places to find accurate information.

Extended Activities:

  1. Have your students write the Chamber of Commence in some city for information.

  2. Arrange for your students to look up designated information on the Internet.

  3. Have your students interview senior citizens in the community for historical information.

Making Decisions

Lesson 47: Gathering Information

1. What information do I need?

2. Where can I find the information?

A. Library.

B. Internet.

C. People.

D. Agencies.

MAKING DECISIONS

Dennis Hanken, Ed.S. and Judith Kennedy, Ed.S.

Lesson 48: Goals—Help You Survive Beyond Today

Objective: Students will set and attain realistic goals.

Materials Needed: None.

Establish the Need: Outline for your students what were your short term and long term goals that you set and met to become a teacher. Elicit input from your students as to what goals they may need to set to attain their goal of preparing themselves for their careers. Be sure to include financial, school, locality, housing, and social support.

Procedures:

Step 1: Model the skill:

Model using "Think Aloud" strategies—setting goals.

1. What goal do I want to reach?
2. Find information about my goal.
3. What steps are needed to reach my goal?
4. Set a time line.
5. Begin.

Helpful Hints: Discuss long-term and short-term goals. How do they differ? Why is each type important?

Step 2: Role play with feedback:

A. Brainstorm ideas for short-term goals.

B. Have each student write a goal and the steps needed to reach it.

Step 3: Transfer training

A. **School:** Have your students set one short-term goal for something school-related.

B. **Home/Community:** Have your students set one goal for home.

C. **Peers:** Have your students set one personal short-term goal with a friend.

Comments: Most financially successful people are goal-oriented. If you live day to day, you are not preparing for the future. Goals are an important part of life.

Extended Activities:

1. Set and discuss a goal for the whole class and the steps needed to get to the goal. Revisit until the goal is met.
2. Have your students write one long-term goal and the steps for accomplishing it.

Making Decisions

Lesson 48:　Goals—Help You Survive Beyond Today

1. What goal do I want to reach?

2. Find information about my goal.

3. What steps are needed to reach my goal?

4. Set a time line.

5. Begin.

MAKING DECISIONS

Lesson 49: Getting Results by Prioritizing

Objective: Students will prioritize personal activities and obligations.

Materials Needed: Journals.

Establish the Need: Read and discuss the following story entitled "Procrastination."

Stephanie wanted to go to the football game with Brianna, but she had a big project due in science tomorrow. She had meant to start the project two weeks ago, but there had been Alex's birthday party and tryouts for the play. Stephanie also liked to spend a lot of time talking. She talked to her friends at school and she would be on the phone all evening if her parents would let her.

1. What is Stephanie's obligation?
2. Has she prioritized her time to have fun and get her obligations done?
3. What are some other choices Stephanie could make or could have made?

Procedures:

Step 1:   Model the skill:

Model using "Think Aloud" strategies—prioritizing activities and obligations.

1. What needs to be accomplished?
2. List your activities from most to least important.
3. Decide the order for doing them.
4. Begin.

Step 2:   Role play with feedback:

Have your students list from most to least important the things they want to accomplish today. Discuss whether they prioritize their time according to what needs to be done.

Step 3:   Transfer training

A. **School:** Lead a discussion with your students on how they can get their school work done and still have time for fun.

B. **Home/Community:** Have them list from most to least important what they want to do at home.

C. **Peers:** Have your students journal ways they can get their other obligations done and still have time for friends.

Comments: Help your students to see that it is often best to get their work done first and then play. The work goes faster when we have something to look forward to. The fun activity is without the burden of pressure because of an unfinished obligation.

Extended Activities:

1. In a class meeting, discuss and prioritize what you want to get done this week, this month, or this year and then set time lines.
2. Identify something which needs attention in your community and prioritize the steps needed to resolve it.

Making Decisions

Lesson 49: Getting Results by Prioritizing

1. What needs to be accomplished?

2. List your activities from most to least important.

3. Decide the order for doing them.

4. Begin.

MAKING DECISIONS

Lesson 50: Problem Solving

Objective: Students will identify the problem and list solutions.

Materials Needed: Ideas for scenarios for step 2.

Establish the Need: Read and discuss the following story entitled "Sean's Test."

Sean got his test paper back. An "F!" How could that be? He was so angry. What would his folks say? That stupid teacher. Didn't he know it wasn't fair to have a test the day after a basketball game? Besides, some of the stuff on the test was out of the book and hadn't been talked about in class.

1. What is the problem?
2. Whose problem is it?
3. Name three possible solutions.

Procedures:

Step 1:   Model the skill:

Model using "Think Aloud" strategies—identifying a problem and listing solutions.

1. What is the problem?
2. Name three possible solutions.
3. Pick the best one and do it.

Step 2:   Role play with feedback:

Role play in groups of four, identifying a problem and listing solutions.

Helpful Hints: Brainstorm with the class some possible problem scenarios such as:

1. You are having so much fun you forget to get home by curfew.
2. You don't allocate time to study for a test and you fail it.
3. You repeat something your friend told you in confidence and now your friend is mad.

Step 3:   Transfer training

A. **School:** (Identify the problem and solutions) The boy in front of you drops his food tray on the floor and the supervisor thinks you did it and yells at you.

B. **Home/Community:** Your little brother gets into your bedroom and messes up your science project.

C. **Peers:** The kids you hang out with are all invited to a party at Brad's. You are not invited.

Comments: The purpose of this lesson is to identify, not only what the problem is, but whose problem it is. If it is the student's problem, that person needs to be responsible and identify several solutions.

Extended Activities:

1. Discuss local current events. Identify problems and solutions.
2. Discuss problems the class has had this year. Identify solutions.
3. Discuss what to do if the problem is very difficult to solve, i.e., go to the counselor, seek adult help, discuss with a parent.

Lesson 50: Problem Solving

1. What is the problem?

2. Name three possible solutions.

3. Pick the best one and do it.

MAKING DECISIONS

Lesson 51: Using Self-Control

Objective: Students will be able to use self-control by recognizing the signs of losing control and then changing their behavior.

Materials Needed: Comic strips from home for extended activity.

Establish the Need: When a person is out of control, what are the fears of the people with him or her? What are the natural consequences? Define and discuss what losing control is. Have you ever seen anyone out of control? Have you ever been out of control? How did each situation make you feel?

Read and discuss the story on the next page entitled "John Lost Control."

Procedures:

Step 1:   Model the skill:

Model using "Think Aloud" strategies.

1. Stop what I am doing.
2. Recognize changes in my body, i.e., tense muscles, rise in body temperature, fidgety or nervousness.
3. What made me feel this way?
4. Think about ways to control myself.
   A. Count to five.
   B. Take deep breaths.
   C. Do something else until I regain control.
5. Weigh my options—make the right choice.

Helpful Hints: Learning to control oneself seems easier for some people than for others.

Gender Differences: Our society portrays men or boys as more aggressive than women or girls. This is probably true in the schools. Boys may be reinforced for this behavior. Girls tend to be aggressive in adolescence, but not to the same degree. Confrontational aggression such as fighting, stealing, vandalism and some school discipline is usually more common with boys. Non-confrontational aggression such as lying, truancy, running away, and substance abuse may be more common with females.

Step 2:   Role play with feedback:

A. Put students in pairs to role play using self-control when they are upset with an adult. Other students watch and give feedback.

B. Have your students demonstrate being in control after a stressful situation at school. Give feedback.

Helpful Hints: Discuss a TV show that illustrates someone losing control. How about pro basketball? Football games? Hockey? Boxing match?

Step 3: **Transfer training**

    A. **School:** You lost your assignments for science class. How do you practice self-control?

    B. **Home/Community:** Your parents won't let you go to a sleep-over. How do you show self-control?

    C. **Peers:** A friend lies to you. How do you show self-control? What is your plan?

Comments: When you are in control of negative emotions, this shows maturity and self-respect. We cannot control how we feel, but we can control our behavior.

Extended Activities:

1. People who commit murder or hurt others show a loss of self-control. Give other examples. Discuss. Point of interest: When you lose control, you cannot process information, you are not rational, and you say and do things that you would not normally do.

2. What are the consequences of losing control?

3. Bring comic strips from home that show examples of characters who show self-control and some that show characters who do not exercise self-control. Discuss the consequences of each.

John Lost Control

When John flunked his science test, he lost control and got mad at his teacher. He not only lost control at school, but he also went home and was upset and mouthed off to his mom.

1. Was John upset with himself or his teacher?
2. What options did he have?
3. Was he upset with his mom?
4. What were some other choices John could have made?

Dennis Hanken, Ed.S. and Judith Kennedy, Ed.S.

Lesson 51: Using Self-Control

1. Stop what I am doing.

2. Recognize the changes in my body, i.e., tense muscles, rise in body temperature, fidgety or nervousness.

3. What made me feel this way?

4. Think about ways to control myself.

   A. Count to five.

   B. Take deep breaths.

   C. Do something else until I regain control.

5. Weigh my options—make the right choice.

HANDLING AGRESSION

Lesson 52: Avoiding Fights

Objective: Students will be able to recognize a conflict and avoid a physical and verbal fight.

Materials Needed: None.

Establish the Need: Paul, a seventh grader, bumped into Will in the hall and knocked him down. Will got up and pushed Paul. Both boys started to push and shove, and then Will hit Paul in the mouth. A teacher came by and sent both boys to the principal.

1. Define the problem.
2. Could they have prevented the fight?
3. Give some alternative ways of handling this problem.

Read and discuss the story, "John Makes a Good Decision," and the fable, "The Lion, the Bear, and the Fox," on the next page.

Procedures:

Step 1:   Model the skill:

Model using "Think Aloud" strategies.

1. Stop and think. Do I want to fight?
2. Choose:
   A. Walk away.
   B. Talk to the person and resolve the problem.
   C. Ask someone to help solve the problem.
   D. Yell for help and run away.
   E. Stand up to the person, if necessary.

Helpful Hints: Discuss the consequences of fighting and hurting someone. Is there peer pressure to fight?

Gender Differences: Boys seem to fight physically more often than girls. Girls may intimidate other girls by threatening or subjecting to social isolation.

Step 2:   Role play with feedback:

A. Using a given scenario (see Helpful Hints), role play, in groups of three, using "Think Aloud" strategies for avoiding fights. Rotate and discuss.

B. Discuss why fighting is not a good solution for solving a problem.

Helpful Hints: Is there ever a time to fight? What about boxing? Scenarios:

1. A rumor is being spread that you hate a certain girl or boy and you want to fight. The student, very hostile, takes you up on the threat to fight and confronts you.

2. Every time you are in the bathroom, a group of kids threatens to beat you up, i.e., they push and shove you and verbally harass you.

3. You found out who stole your CD player from your locker. When you ask for it back, the student accuses you of lying and starts a physical fight with you.

Step 3:	**Transfer training**

    A. **School:** Discuss avoiding fights in school. Where and when do fights occur? What can you do to avoid fights?

    B. **Home/Community:** Is there a place you need to stay away from in your town to avoid fights?

    C. **Peers:** Some students like to fight. How do you avoid these students?

Comments: Sometimes the way to avoid fights is to avoid certain people and places. What can you do when you can't avoid them?

Extended Activities:

1. Some people grow up in an environment that promotes physical aggression. Fighting may be a way of life. How do you deal with this issue? Counseling, discussion, parent training—what can change this frame of mind?

2. Make a list of ways to avoid fighting.

3. Take a vote in class: How many people have ever been in a physical fight?

4. Write a rap citing ways to avoid fights

John Makes a Good Decision

John, the biggest and toughest kid in the eighth grade, was always fighting and didn't fear anyone. One day he pushed a seventh grader around. This boy, Steve, had an older brother who waited after school for John. He confronted John about pushing Steve. John backed down and decided not to fight. Good decision! He finally realized he doesn't have to fight everyone. He made a good choice. He started having more friends and liked himself better.

AESOP's Fable: The Lion, the Bear, and the Fox

A lion and a bear found the carcass of a fawn. Both were hungry. Both wanted it. So they started to fight for it. The contest was long, hard, and savage. At last, when both of them—half blinded and half dead—lay panting on the ground without the strength to touch the prize before them, a fox came by.

Noting the helpless condition of the two beasts, the impudent fox stepped nimbly between them, seized the fawn over which they had battled, and with never a "thank you," dragged it away to his den.

Application: Only fools fight to exhaustion while a rogue runs off with the dinner.

Educational Media Corporation®, Box 21311, Minneapolis, MN 55421-0311

Handling Aggression

Lesson 52: Avoiding Fights

1. **Stop and think.**
   Do I want to fight?

2. **Choose:**

   A. **Walk away.**

   B. **Talk to the person and resolve the problem.**

   C. **Ask someone to help solve the problem.**

   D. **Yell for help and run away.**

   E. **Stand up to the person, if necessary.**

HANDLING AGRESSION

Lesson 53: Avoiding Trouble with Others

Objective: Students will be able to recognize a bad situation and make a good choice to avoid trouble.

Materials Needed: None.

Establish the Need: Some people avoid bad situations by thinking about right and wrong. Others are more impulsive; they act first and think about it later. Which are you?

Procedures:

Step 1:   Model the skill:

Model using "Think Aloud" strategies.

1. Assess the situation.

2. Is it a good or bad situation?

3. Choose:

   A. Negotiate.

   B. Compromise.

   C. Walk away.

Step 2:   Role play with feedback:

A. You hang around with a group of kids. They all decide to steal CDs from a store. Role play what you would do, using the "Think Aloud" strategies. Discuss.

B. Your best friend wants you to help him or her cheat on a test. You don't want to. Discuss and role play! Use "Think Aloud" strategies.

Step 3:   Transfer training

A. **School:** Your friends ask you to tease someone they don't like. Should you join them?

B. **Home/Community:** A local hangout for students is often raided by the police. Should you go there?

C. **Peers:** Your best friends want you to steal some cigarettes from home and bring them to a hiding place and smoke. What do you do?

Comments: Peer pressure is **very** powerful. You have to be very secure to say "no."

Extended Activities:

1. Make a list of bad situations in school.

2. As a group, act out a spontaneous play using different situations. Choose one play where the characters avoid trouble and then one where they don't. Discuss the consequences of each.

Handling Aggression

Lesson 53: Avoiding Trouble with Others

1. Assess the situation.

2. Is it a good or bad situation?

3. Choose:

A. Negotiate.

B. Compromise.

C. Walk away.

HANDLING AGRESSION

Lesson 54: Responding to Intimidation

Objective: Students will be able to recognize intimidation or bullying and respond to it in an appropriate manner.

Materials Needed: Story from *AESOP's Fables*.

Establish the Need: Read the following story entitled "The Wolf and The Lamb."

As a wolf was lapping at the head of a running brook, he spied a lamb daintily paddling his feet some distance down the stream. "There's my supper," thought the wolf. "But I'll have to find some excuse for attacking such a harmless creature." So he shouted down at the lamb, "How dare you stir up the water I am drinking and make it muddy?" "But you must be mistaken," bleated the lamb. "How can I be spoiling your water, since it runs from you to me and not from me to you?" "Don't argue," snapped the wolf. "I know you. You are the one who was saying those ugly things about me behind my back a year ago." "Oh, sir," replied the lamb, trembling, "a year ago I was not even born." "Well," snarled the wolf, "if it was not you, then it was your father, and that amounts to the same thing. Besides, I'm not going to have you argue me out of my supper." Without another word he fell upon the helpless lamb and tore her to pieces.

Application: Any excuse will serve a tyrant.

1. What does intimidation mean?

2. What is the example of intimidation in this story?

Read and discuss the story on the next page entitled "Mark, The Bully."

Procedures:

Step 1:   **Model the skill:**

Model using "Think Aloud" strategies.

1. Stop and think—Is this person trying to intimidate me?

2. What are my choices:

A. Walk away.

B. Ignore.

C. Defend myself.

D. Tell an adult.

3. Try not to show fear.

4. After the incident, process with an adult.

Helpful Hints: Most of the time bullies are bigger students who pick on smaller students. They rely on fear and size. Most bullies will leave students their own size alone. Do you know a bully in your grade?

Gender Differences: Most bullies are boys. What about girls? Are gossip, peer pressure, control, and manipulation forms of bullying? Do bullies pick on the students they perceive as weaker? Is there a policy in your school for when this occurs? What about your neighborhood?

Step 2:　Role play with feedback:

  A. Role play in small groups. Have each student take the role of the bully and also the victim. Discuss. Rotating the roles is important.

  B. Role play the bully on the bus or after school on the way home from school. Discuss.

Step 3:　Transfer training

  A. **School:** A bigger older student keeps shoving you around at lunch. What should you do?

  B. **Home/Community:** A boy across the street wants to fight you. He is very persistent. What do you do?

  C. **Peers:** One of your best friends wants to wrestle all the time. He usually wins and you have to say "uncle." What do you do?

Comments: Most students will encounter a bully or two in their lifetime. Assertive behavior is considered the best plan to deal with bullies.

Extended Activities:

1. In the big picture, how would you assess a person who gives people a difficult time, i.e., banker, rich person, politician? It doesn't always have to end in a physical fight. Maybe your parents could name some. What if you posted their names and pictures in the office and called them bullies, would that help? Does peer pressure work?

2. Rank the following values individually and then as a class. Rank the values as to their importance to you with #1 being the most important and #10 being the least important. Discuss.

Safety	Health
New Car	Good Grades
Friends	Money
Getting Even	Showing I'm Tough
Being Kind	Having Fun

Mark, The Bully

Mark was the biggest kid in the seventh grade. He picked on the boys and made girls uncomfortable with his comments. One day a new student moved in, and he was even bigger than Mark. He was also a bigger bully than Mark. Mark started to see himself in the new student and didn't like what he saw. He not only changed, but he challenged the new student to change. Mark wasn't very successful with changing the new student, but he was more likable and understanding of his fellow students.

Handling Aggression

Lesson 54: Responding to Intimidation

1. Stop and think—Is this person trying to intimidate me?

2. What are my choices:

   A. Walk away.

   B. Ignore.

   C. Defend myself.

   D. Tell an adult.

3. Try not to show fear.

4. After the incident, process with an adult.

HANDLING AGRESSION

Lesson 55: Expressing Anger in Appropriate Ways

Objective: Students will be able to express anger in appropriate ways.

Materials Needed: None.

Establish the Need: Read the stories that follow this lesson. Discuss.

Anger could be defined as: a feeling of extreme displeasure, hostility, indignation, or exasperation toward someone or something. Synonyms are: rage, fury, ire, wrath, and resentment. Anger is an emotion which is neither good or bad. How you act on your anger is determined by how you were socialized—what you learned about how to act when you felt angry. Read and discuss "Some Ways to Respond to Anger" on page 159.

Read and discuss the stories on pages 157-158 entitled "Sibling Rivalry" and "The Fence."

Procedures:

Step 1:   Model the skill:

Model using "Think Aloud" strategies—a situation in which you are angry.

1. Stop and breathe slowly.
2. Time yourself out—walk away.
3. Ask why am I really angry?
4. What is my goal?
5. Reengage when appropriate.

Helpful Hints and Gender Differences: Anger knows no boundaries. Boys and girls can both lose control. In our society it might be tolerated more from boys, especially when exhibited in sports. Girls are less likely to show anger in a physical way. Remember, anger interferes with information processing and attention. Anger is a normal emotion. Our behavior when we are angry is what we can control.

Step 2:   Role play with feedback:

A. Role play in groups of three using different scenarios (see Helpful Hints). Use "Think Aloud" strategies. Discuss the results.

B. Journal what makes you angry and what happens when you get angry. Do comparisons when you are in control and not in control.

Helpful Hints: Suggested scenarios:

1. Your best friend is always flirting with the girl or boy you like.
2. Your parents blame you for anything that goes wrong with your brother or sister.
3. You lost your homework.
4. You're late for school.

5. You are being teased and called names.

6. You lost the $20 that your parents gave you for lunch money.

Step 3: **Transfer training**

A. **School:** Can you express your anger to your teacher in an appropriate way? Give examples from the past.

B. **Home/Community:** Most homes have some conflict. Reflect on a recent incident. How does your family handle anger?

C. **Peers:** When you get mad at a friend, what happens? Discuss how your friends handle conflict and anger.

Comments: Anger can be a powerful manipulative weapon. Prisons are full of angry people who couldn't control their anger. It is important for students to learn that feeling angry is okay and normal. What we can control is how we express our anger.

Extended Activities:

1. Make a list of all the different ways people handle their anger. In our society, does having lawyers help? What are some ways of taking responsibility for your actions? When you get mad and people back off, does that reinforce your using anger again?

2. Journal all the things that make you angry. How do you handle anger? What are some other ways you could handle feeling angry?

Sibling Rivalry

John and Bob were brothers. Bob was older and liked to pick on John. One day Bob was teasing John, and John hit and cursed Bob for five minutes. Finally Bob hit John really hard and cracked his front teeth. Their parents were really mad and blamed Bob because he was the oldest.

1. Should parents always blame the oldest?

2. What consequence should they both receive?

3. What are some ways both John and Bob could control their anger?

Handling Aggression

The Fence

There was a little boy with a bad temper. His father gave him a bag of nails and told him that every time he lost his temper, to hammer a nail in the back fence. The first day the boy had driven 37 nails into the fence. Then it gradually dwindled down. He discovered it was easier to hold his temper than to drive those nails into the fence. Finally the day came when the boy didn't lose his temper at all. He told his father about it and the father suggested that the boy now pull out one nail for each day that he was able to hold his temper. The days passed and the young boy was finally able to tell his father that all the nails were gone. The father took his son by the hand and led him to the fence. He said, You have done well, my son, but look at the holes in the fence. The fence will never be the same. When you say things in anger, they leave a scar just like this one. You can put a knife in a man and draw it out. It won't matter how many times you say "I'm sorry," the wound is still there. A verbal wound is as bad as a physical one.

Author Unknown

Some Ways to Respond to Anger*

1. Angry people want to be heard. Listen to what they have to say. They need to be heard because they tend to think they are being ignored.

2. Angry people want someone to notice their feelings—acknowledge their feelings. Don't try to talk them out of feeling angry.

3. Angry people want someone to see their point of view. You can argue that the person has a good reason for being angry, but you need to try to focus on solving the problem.

4. Angry people may want help in figuring out what caused the anger. We may be able to negotiate with them when they calm down and then try to problem solve.

5. Angry people want respect. Each person needs to be heard and then process through to resolution.

6. Angry people do not process information well. After the strongest feelings have subsided, you may collect and share information.

7. Angry people need to know that they are accepted. It is best to end angry confrontations on a positive note.

8. Angry people need to know that any effort to help them is sincere. Some people who have major anger issues may have to revisit situations over and over to bring about change.

*Myers and Nance (1986)

Lesson 55: Expressing Anger in Appropriate Ways

1. Stop and breathe slowly.

2. Time yourself out—walk away.

3. Ask why am I really angry?

4. What is my goal?

5. Reengage when appropriate.

HANDLING AGRESSION

Lesson 56: Negotiating / Compromising

Objective: Students will recognize differences of opinion and negotiate without arguing.

Materials Needed: None.

Establish the Need: As a class, define the words "Compromise" and "Negotiate.. What are some examples currently in the news that involve compromise and negotiation? What may happen if people refuse to compromise? Read and discuss the story on the next page entitled "Beth Compromises."

Procedures:

Step 1:   Model the skill:

Model using "Think Aloud" strategies.

1. Are we disagreeing?
2. Tell the other person my opinion without put downs.
3. Ask the other person's opinion.
4. Listen respectfully.
5. Think about the feelings and opinions of the other person.
6. Can I compromise?

Helpful Hints: People compromise every day of their lives. List examples.

Step 2:   Role play with feedback:

A. Role play, in small groups, negotiating differences of opinion. Rotate and discuss. Some topics: Boys are smarter than girls, girls are more creative, poverty is resolvable, violence in our school is under control, who should pay on dates?

B. Role play again with boys on one side, girls on the other. How does this change opinions?

Helpful Hints: Can you compromise when you discuss religion, politics, dating at 14 not 16? What happens when you won't compromise?

Step 3:   Transfer training

A. **School:** You and your teacher disagree about when the test should be given. Negotiate. You and your teacher disagree about you having turned in an assignment.

B. **Home/Community:** You are fighting over what show to watch on TV. Negotiate.

C. **Peers:** You want to go to different movies on Friday night. Negotiate.

Comments: It's okay to have different opinions, values, and beliefs. However, being closed minded can label you as stubborn or opinionated. Discuss. What are some examples of times a person might choose not to compromise?

Extended Activities: 1. What professions use this skill everyday?

Develop a skit on passing a bill in Congress. Give the pros and cons.

2. Following is a list of circumstances. Identify which ones you could choose to negotiate and which ones you couldn't.

A. A group wants you to steal from a convenience store.

Negotiate? Why or why not?

B. Your friend adamantly believes smoking doesn't hurt you.

Negotiate? Why or why not?

C. You want to go the movies; your friend wants to go to the mall.

Negotiate? Why or why not?

D. You need to study for a test; some friends want to go to the lake.

Negotiate? Why or why not?

E. A friend wants you to try drugs.

Negotiate? Why or why not?

F. A friend ridicules your new hair cut and tells you to change it.

Negotiate? Why or why not?

Beth Compromises

Beth had a disagreement with her teacher on the answer to an essay question on a science test. Neither would give an inch. Beth said it was the difference between an A and a B grade. Beth was able to justify her answer from a point of view that her teacher had not considered. Her teacher decided there was validity to Beth's way of responding. She negotiated with Beth and gave her credit for her answer.

1. Do you think Beth is stubborn?

2. Do you think the teacher was threatened by Beth?

3. Was the ending solution-based?

Lesson 56: Negotiating / Compromising

1. Are we disagreeing?

2. Tell the other person my opinion without put downs.

3. Ask the other person's opinion.

4. Listen respectfully.

5. Think about the feelings and opinion of the other person.

6. Can I compromise?

HANDLING AGRESSION

Lesson 57: Handling Feelings of Anger and Sadness

Objective: Students will realize they are feeling angry or sad and deal with their feelings in an appropriate way.

Materials Needed: None.

Establish the Need: Some people seem to be angry all the time. They seem to have a "chip" on their shoulder. Maybe they're mad at being poor, dislike their parents, can't fit into groups, aren't very athletic, or very cute. There are thousands of reasons people can feel bad. Some of us try to bury these feelings deep inside ourselves. Others take their feelings out on our closest friends, parents, or siblings. Somehow we have to handle these feelings, or they may lead to physical problems and negative thoughts and actions. Remember the characters in Charles Dickens' *A Christmas Carol?* Scrooge is mad all the time—negative and stingy. Why do you think he feels this way? Do people want to be around others who are negative all the time?

Procedures:

Step 1:   Model the skill:

Model using "Think Aloud" strategies.

1. What am I feeling?

2. How am I dealing with it?

3. What can I do to change my actions?

   A. Make a plan to change my behavior.

   B. Talk to adults and friends about my problem.

   C. Am I over reacting?

   D. Do I need to talk with a mental health professional?

   E. Make a choice and take action.

Gender Differences: Boys may act out their anger, while girls may internalize it. One way to express anger is to talk about it. It is unhealthy to store it up and ruminate about it. Other healthy ways to handle anger and sadness are exercise and journaling. Stress to your students that they should seek professional help if they are unable to handle their feelings on their own.

Step 2:   Role play with feedback:

A. Journal about the last time you were angry or sad. What did you do and how did you feel?

B. Journal how your family deals with anger. What happens when Dad gets mad? What happens when Mother gets mad? How about your siblings?

Helpful Hints: How does environment affect how we deal with anger? It may be new information to your students that anger or irritability is one of the most reliable symptoms of depression.

Step 3:   Transfer training

A. **School:** A friend of yours has been gossiping about you being the teacher's pet. How do you handle this?

B. **Home/Community:** Your brother is sneaking in to your room and reading your diary. What do you do?

C. **Peers:** Your best friend borrows things and seldom returns them. What do you do?

Comments: This lesson is meant to assist students with handling anger. What happens next? Sometimes people express their anger right away. Sometimes they are unaware of why they are feeling angry or sad. This lesson explores healthy ways to deal with anger and sadness.

Extended Activities:

1. Identify any long-term problems you live with that cause feelings of anger or sadness. People do not always realize that living with disability, illness, poverty, violence, shame, and ridicule can cause long-term feelings of anger or sadness.

2. Have the nurse, counselor, or some other knowledgeable person come to your class and talk about the medications that help with long-term feelings of anger or sadness. Have that person describe the medical condition of depression.

Handling Aggression

Lesson 57: Handling Feelings of Anger and Sadness

1. What am I feeling?

2. How am I dealing with it?

3. What can I do to change my actions?

   A. Make a plan to change my behavior.

   B. Talk to adults and friends about my problem.

   C. Am I over reacting?

   D. Do I need to talk with a mental health professional?

   E. Make a choice and take action.

HANDLING AGRESSION

Lesson 58: Signs of Depression

Objective: Students will be able to recognize signs of depression and move to a plan of action or seek professional help.

Materials Needed: Counselors available.

Establish the Need: Read the symptoms on page 169, having your students self-evaluate the presence or absence of symptoms. Depression, a medical illness, is comprised of a multitude of symptoms that reliably co-occur. If any person who is usually outgoing, pleasant, and happy changes to feeling moody, sad, and irritable, this constituents a major change in that person's lifestyle. It is not a phase or adolescent characteristic. The major signs of depression are: (People are considered to be clinically depressed if they have five to six of these symptoms).

Tell your students that if they have five or six of these symptoms (for at least two to three months), they may have depression and should see one of the counselors you have available. Handle this discreetly.

Procedures:

Step 1:   Model the skill:

Model using "Think Aloud" strategies.

1. Do I have five or more signs of depression?
2. If yes.
3. Seek professional help:
   A. School counselor.
   B. Community counselor.
   C. Any adult who can help or show me where to go for help.
   D. Family doctor.
4. Be honest about my feelings.
5. Ask for support from family and friends.

Gender Differences: About an equal number of boys and girls are identified as depressed in school-age children, ages 9 to 18. Boys can show aggression as a symptom of depression. When in doubt about yourself, ask for help. Sometimes parents and teachers don't recognize the signs of depression.

Depression is misunderstood by many to be a state of unhappiness that the person can snap out of. Depression is a serious medical problem that needs professional attention.

Step 2:   Role play with feedback:

A. Role play how one might feel or act in a typical school day if depressed. Discuss.
B. Discuss ways to help others who seem depressed.

Helpful Hints: The age group 9 to 13 is the fastest growing age group for depression. Children with learning difficulties seem more likely to have depression, as that is one more stress in their lives. Antidepressants have few side effects and are warranted in long term depression.

Step 3:   Transfer training

    A. **School:** If you know someone who has threatened suicide or is depressed, tell a school counselor or teacher.

    B. **Home/Community:** Is there a history of depression in your family or someone currently on medication? Discuss with your family.

    C. **Peers:** Have any of your friends been depressed? How did you react when you heard about it?

Comments: *Childhood Depression* by Kevin Stark (Guilford Press) is an excellent resource for teachers because it has school-based interventions. Teachers should let school counselors know if they suspect a student is depressed or shows several signs of depression. Be sure to have well informed counselors available to talk with any student who needs to talk.

Extended Activities:

1. Journal how you handle your feelings of sadness.
2. In your journal, list ongoing stressful events that may adversely affect you.
3. Have the class brainstorm all the community resources that are available to deal with depression.
4. Consider having a medical doctor come to class and discuss depression.

Signs of Depression

1. Sadness or depressed. This is found in 70% of depressed children (Carlson & Cantwell, 1982). Especially if the child is sad for at least 3 hours a day, 5 days a week, for the last 15 weeks.

2. Angry or irritable mood.

3. Anhedonia—loss of the pleasure response, might be bored over half of his or her waking hours or no longer has pleasure from over half of his or her activities.

4. Weepy—tends to cry more.

5. Loss of mirth response—less capable of responding to humor.

6. Feeling unloved—a perception that no one loves him or her.

7. Self-pity—feels life is unfair or less fulfilling.

8. Negative self-evaluation—low self-esteem.

9. Guilt—blames things on self.

10. Hopelessness—no hope of things getting better.

11. Difficulty concentrating—can't make decisions or concentrate in school.

12. Indecisiveness—difficulty making or sticking with decisions.

13. Morbid ideation—preoccupied with death.

14. Social withdrawal—decline in the frequency of contact and depth of involvement with adults and children.

15. Suicide ideation and behavior—thinking about killing oneself.

16. Decreased academic performance.

17. Fatigue—feeling of being tired or lacking energy.

18. Change in appetite and/or weight—either a decline in appetite or feels like eating all the time.

19. Aches and pains—physical complaints.

20. Sleep disturbance—insomnia or hypersomnia.

21. Motor retardation—slowing down of bodily movements, speed, or reaction times.

22. Motor agitation—unable to sit still, acting out.

Handling Aggression

Lesson 58: Signs of Depression

1. Do I have five or more signs of depression?

2. If yes.

3. Seek Professional help:

   A. School counselor.

   B. Community counselor.

   C. Any adult who can help or show me where to go for help.

   D. Family doctor.

4. Be honest about my feelings.

5. Ask for support from family and friends.

HANDLING AGRESSION

Lesson 59: Troubled Adolescents— What to Look For and What to Do

Objective: Students will be able to recognize a troubled classmate and either give support or notify an adult to lend support.

Materials Needed: Counselors available.

Establish the Need: All children experience problems at one time or another. Some problems are handled right away, and some linger and cross over into school and affect the way they learn.

Some examples of children who need help:

1. Children who experiment with drugs, are listless, or are having trouble focusing in school.
2. Children who are being abused or neglected.
3. Children who are in gangs.
4. Children who have talked about suicide.
5. Children who have threatened others with physical harm.
6. Children who say they want to blow up the school or hurt teachers or other students.
7. Children who have strange thoughts or act in bizarre ways.
8. Children who are constantly negative and hate school.

Comments: These are some examples. There are many more. Some of the these students can be helped by counseling or educational interventions. Parents need to be involved from the start of the problem.

Procedures:

Step 1:   Model the skill:

Model using "Think Aloud" strategies.

1. Recognize there is a problem.
2. Consider options and take appropriate action.

    A. Report to the proper professional.

    B. Talk to the student.

    C. Talk to the student's parents.

    D. Contact the crisis team.

Helpful Hints: Recognize that this person needs help, but may not recognize it. Parents need to know as soon as possible. Schools that have support teams can help intervene. Students who know about problems and don't respond can be held liable in some cases. (Bomb threats etc.) A safe school is the responsibility of all of its members.

Step 2: **Role play with feedback:**

    A. Role play a situation in which you know about a student who is threatening a teacher. Discuss.

    B. Role play how you would react if you heard about a bomb threat. What are your responsibilities? Discuss.

Step 3: **Transfer training**

    A. **School:** You know a classmate has a weapon in his or her backpack. What's your plan of action?

    B. **Home/Community:** Your father has abused your younger brother or sister. What's your plan of action?

    C. **Peers:** A friend says she wants to commit suicide. What should you do?

Helpful Hints: Turning your back on a major problem is not an appropriate action. Ask adults for guidance.

Comments: Tell your students it is not betrayal if they seek help for a friend.

Extended Activities:

1. Make a list of things that have occurred in schools that could have been prevented. Can you blame schools and teachers for students' actions? Discuss.

2. Can there be a "Dear Abby" kind of format for kids to write to anonymously for help?

3. Write a short skit with your students to help them see different situations where depression can develop and how it manifests itself.

Lesson 59: Troubled Adolescents— What to Look For & What to Do

1. Recognize there is a problem.

2. Consider options and take appropriate action.

   A. Report to the proper professional.

   B. Talk to the student.

   C. Talk to the student's parents.

   D. Contact the crisis team.

HANDLING AGRESSION

Lesson 60: Grieving

Objective: Students will be able to grieve the loss of a family member, friend, or school staff member or support someone who is grieving in an appropriate manner.

Materials Needed: Have counselors available.

Establish the Need: In the course of a school career, most students will encounter the death of a classmate, a relative, or a school staff member. Some students will be able to deal with this issue and others will have a very difficult time with it. Our society does not always model effective grieving. Grieving is a very difficult process and differs, depending on the age of the child. Death is not talked about in everyday social circles. Yet death is a part of being a human being; we all will die. Most of us think death happens when people are old. That is why death is so tragic when it occurs at an early age. People have different beliefs about what happens after we die. When accidents or suicides occur, it is difficult for the immediate families and friends to accept. A good support system is needed for all involved to come to resolution and acceptance. For some people, therapy is recommended to accept the death of a friend or spouse.

Procedures:

Step 1: Model the skill:

Model using "Think Aloud" strategies.

1. Has the person suffered a loss?
2. What can I do?
   A. Say, "I'm sorry."
   B. Do something for that person.
   C. Consider attending the funeral.
   D. Suggest professional help, if necessary.

Step 2: Role play with feedback:

A. Role play expressing grief to someone who has had a loss.

B. Role play how you reacted to a death in your family or the death of your friend. What were the long term effects? How long did you grieve?

Step 3: Transfer training

A. **School:** Discuss the death of a student. How would this affect classmates? What would be the climate of the class for a week?

B. **Home/Community:** Discuss the death of a relative. The length of the grieving might depend on how close you were.

C. **Peers:** Discuss the death of a friend or how would you feel if a friend died suddenly.

Helpful Hints: Five Stages of Grief: (Kubler-Ross)

1. Denial 2. Anger 3. Bargaining 4. Depression 5. Acceptance

Comments: Discuss suicide or death from drugs. When a death occurs, support the family and close friends. Say to them, "I am sorry about your loss." You might offer to watch children, cook a meal, or whatever. Be there for them. Don't stay silent or say, "I know what your going though, call me if you need something." Respect the family. You shouldn't ask about how the person died or ask them how they feel. Be supportive and loving, not nosy. Respect their feelings by letting them talk about their memories or anything they want. Grieving is an individual process. It may take years to get over a death. Allow each individual to take his or her time. Respect their privacy. If you can tell that they are not getting over a death, you could suggest therapy.

Extended Activities:

1. Discuss the death of a famous person who died recently. Discuss the different reactions.

2. Define support. Support means listening, holding, giving food, and so forth.

3. Have a counselor come to your class and discuss grieving.

4. Most people want to talk with others about the person who died.

Lesson 60: Grieving

1. Has the person suffered a loss?

2. What can I do?

   A. Say, "I'm sorry."

   B. Do something for that person.

   C. Consider attending the funeral.

   D. Suggest professional help, if necessary.

HANDLING AGRESSION

Lesson 61: Staying Positive About Myself

Objective: Students will list their strengths.

Materials Needed: Journals.

Establish the Need: Read and discuss the following story entitled "How Do I Look?"

Julie looked in the mirror. She saw a face with pimples, hair that didn't look right, and a body that was too fat. She didn't look anything like those girls in *Seventeen*. No wonder she didn't have any friends! She probably wouldn't even get asked to dance tonight at the dance.

1. Is there anyone who has no good qualities?
2. Is it hard for you to state your good qualities?
3. Discuss that even "super models" have qualities they dislike about themselves.

Procedures:

Step 1:   Model the skill:

Model using "Think Aloud" strategies—list on the board your good qualities.

1. What am I good at?
2. What do I like about myself?
3. What do others like about me?

Step 2:   Role play with feedback:

A. In journals, have your students list at least five good qualities about themselves.
B. In pairs, have them share one of those five qualities with each other.

Helpful Hints: Some students really struggle with self-esteem problems; therefore, affirmations may be helpful. You might assign your students the task of saying aloud, to oneself in the mirror, one positive statement each day, such as, "I am calm and confident."

Step 3:   Transfer training

A. **School:** Journal what I am good at in school.
B. **Home/Community:** What am I good at, at home?
C. **Peers:** In what ways am I a good friend?

Comments: This would be a good time to lead a class discussion on the qualities of a good friend. The qualities of a good student.

Extended Activities:

1. Write a short story stating the things that you do well.
2. Pair your students and have them say one thing they like about the other person.
3. Have all of your students come up with one word to describe themselves. Then make a collage out of those words. (The words must be positive.)

Lesson 61: Staying Positive About Myself

1. What am I good at?

2. What do I like about myself?

3. What do others like about me?

SELF-ACCEPTANCE

Dennis Hanken, Ed.S. and Judith Kennedy, Ed.S.

Lesson 62: Making Mistakes—A Way to Grow

Objective: Students will state one thing they could learn from a mistake.

Materials Needed: Scenarios of mistakes for step 2 written on paper or on the board. (See Comments)

Establish the Need: Read and discuss the following:

Robby wanted to go out for track. He decided he would start running every day in January to get in shape. He set his alarm to get up early to run before school. When it went off at 5:30, Robby dragged himself out of bed. He looked out the window. It was still dark and it had snowed! He climbed back into bed and pulled the covers over his head. Morning after morning Robby found an excuse not to go running. At tryouts for track, Robby got off to a great start, but he soon became winded and fell behind.

1. What was Robby's mistake?

2. What could he learn from this mistake?

Procedures:

Step 1: Model the skill:

Model using "Think Aloud" strategies—getting a ticket for not having current license plates.

1. What is my mistake?

2. What can I learn from it?

Step 2: Role play with feedback:

Group your students in fours, hand out the mistake scenarios, and have them identify the mistakes and what could be learned from it.

Step 3: Transfer training

A. **School:** Ask the PE teacher to help students see their mistakes and what they can learn from them.

B. **Home/Community:** You don't get all your projects done for your scout badge. What do you do?

C. **Peers:** You want to hang out with a specific group of kids, but they shun you. What do you do?

Comments: Some possible scenarios:

1. I went to a movie, rather than staying home to study for a test.

2. I repeated a secret my best friend had told me in confidence.

3. I was trying to impress my friends, drove too fast, and got a speeding ticket.

Extended Activities:

1. Elicit a discussion from your students of examples when people in history or literature made a mistake and learned from it.

2. Journal about past mistakes and what you learned from them.

Lesson 62: Making Mistakes—
A Way to Grow

1. What is my mistake?

2. What can I learn from it?

SELF-ACCEPTANCE

Lesson 63: Handling "Put Downs"

Objective: Students will ignore disparaging remarks from others.

Materials Needed: Scenarios for put downs. (See Helpful Hints)

Establish the Need: Read and discuss the following story entitled "Cruel Remarks Hurt."

Tom seemed to enjoy telling others they were stupid, fat, clumsy, or ugly. Sometimes he would get others to join him in taunting another person. Tom especially liked it if the person he made fun of got upset.

1. How do you feel when you are put down?
2. Why do some people make cruel remarks?
3. What are the best ways to handle mean remarks?

Procedures:

Step 1:   Model the skill:

Model using "Think Aloud" strategies—handling put downs.

1. Is what the person says mean and untrue?
2. What can I do?
   A. Ignore.
   B. Speak up.
   C. Avoid.

Helpful Hints: Help your students to see that those who put down others do not feel good about themselves.

Step 2:   Role play with feedback:

In small groups, have your students role play scenarios for put downs.

Helpful Hints: Scenarios could include: calling names, remarks about others' character or physical features, remarks about one's ethnicity, sexual orientation, or family.

Step 3:   Transfer training

A. **School:** Ask other teachers to watch for put downs and handle them immediately.

B. **Home/Community:** Ask your students to watch for put downs and report back how people handle them.

C. **Peers:** Make a contract with your students that they will not participate in put downs.

Comments: Research indicates that put downs are one level of violence. In a safe school environment, it is important to stop put downs.

Extended Activities:

1. Journal how you feel when others put you down and when you put others down.
2. In groups, have your students develop skits on handling put downs.

Self Acceptance

Lesson 63: Handling "Put Downs"

1. Is what the person says mean and untrue?

2. What can I do?

A. Ignore.

B. Speak up.

C. Avoid.

SELF-ACCEPTANCE

Dennis Hanken, Ed.S. and Judith Kennedy, Ed.S.

Lesson 64: Doing Your Best

Objective: Students will try even if the task is hard.

Materials Needed: Props for various physical activities, such as: a ball (to try to balance on end of finger), a saucer (in which to try to throw a coin), an egg (to balancing on one end).

Establish the Need: Have your students try various tasks that will be very difficult for some, such as: tossing coin into saucer and getting it to stay there, balancing a ball on one finger, balancing an egg on one end, repeating a series of eight numbers. Have fun with this. The objective is to show that all people have trouble with some things, but it is important to try one's best at necessary tasks.

Procedures:

| Step 1: | Model the skill: |

Model using "Think Aloud" strategies—doing your best at something difficult (might be juggling three objects).

1. Can I do the task?
2. What will happen if I do/do not try?
3. Visualize myself successfully doing the task.
4. Try my best.

| Step 2: | Role play with feedback: |

Have your students try their best to do a new activity. It could be a math concept, memory activity, juggling activity, and so forth.

| Step 3: | Transfer training |

A. **School:** Ask the PE teacher to reinforce doing your best.

B. **Home/Community:** Have your students journal something they could do their best at home.

C. **Peers:** Lead a class in discussion of what it means to do your best as a friend.

Comments: Each person can do something unique. Show off your talents.

Extended Activities:

1. Have your students research someone's life, i.e., athlete, politician, philanthropist, and report back examples how that person tried to do his or her best.

2. Have them journal about a time in their lives when they tried to do their best. What were the results?

Lesson 64: Doing Your Best

1. Can I do the task?

2. What will happen if I do/do not try?

3. Visualize myself successfully doing the task.

4. Try my best.

SELF-ACCEPTANCE

Dennis Hanken, Ed.S. and Judith Kennedy, Ed.S.

Lesson 65: Put Ups

Objective: Students will make positive remarks to self and others.

Materials Needed: Journal.

Establish the Need: Read and discuss the following story entitled "Being Positive."

Luke seemed to be able to see the best in people. He would say, "Good job!" to people on his team who made a good play, or, "Nice try" to someone who made a good effort. He did not join in when other kids made rude remarks to each other. People seemed to feel better when Luke was around.

1. Why did people like to be around Luke?

2. Does it take any more energy to make positive remarks than negative ones?

Procedures:

Step 1:   Model the skill:

Model using "Think Aloud" strategies—giving a put up to someone.

1. What can I say I like about the person?

2. Say it.

Helpful Hints: Be sure to tell your students that it is important to be truthful, as well as positive. Insincere compliments are shallow.

Step 2:   Role play with feedback:

In pairs, have your students take turns giving each other a "put up."

Step 3:   Transfer training

A. **School:** Ask other teachers to give your students "put ups" this week.

B. **Home/Community:** Send a note to parents telling them what the lesson is and ask them to give "put ups" this week.

C. **Peers:** Assign every student to give three "put ups" each day to others.

Comments: Research states that people learn best in environments that have at least five "put ups" for every "put down."

Extended Activities:

1. Journal how you feel when you get "put ups." How do you feel when you get "put downs?"

2. Create a skit for younger grades showing the power of "put ups."

3. Create a game incorporating giving opponents "put ups."

4. Why do students become jealous of popular students? Are positive students popular? Why?

Self Acceptance

Lesson 65: Put Ups

1. What can I say I like about the person?

2. Say it.

SELF-ACCEPTANCE

       Dennis Hanken, Ed.S. and Judith Kennedy, Ed.S.

Lesson 66: Handling the Ups and Downs

Objective: Students will state three things they can do when things are going well for them, and three things they can do when things are not going well.

Materials Needed: Journal.

Establish the Need: Read and discuss the following:

Theodore Roosevelt is famous for saying, "When the going gets tough, the tough get going."

1. What do you think that means?
2. What are some things you can do when the going gets tough?

Procedures:

Step 1:   Model the skill:

Model using "Think Aloud" strategies—what to do when the going gets tough.

1. Why are things tough for me right now?
2. What are three things I can do?
3. Pick one and try it.
4. Pick another, if necessary, and try it.

Helpful Hints: Mental health experts state that people need to see at least three options in a situation in order to get out of either/or dichotomy thinking.

Step 2:   Role play with feedback:

In groups, have your students role play using "Think Aloud" strategies—how to handle a tough situation. Brainstorm with them some examples of "tough" situations.

Step 3:   Transfer training

A. **School:** Lead a class in discussion of how to handle tough situations at school.
B. **Home/Community:** Have your students journal ways to handle tough situations at home.
C. **Peers:** In groups, have them list ways to handle tough situations with peers, such as: bullying, exclusion, group pressure, teasing, and gangs.

Comments: Discuss fair and unfair. Some days are better than others.

Extended Activities:

1. Write short stories depicting a tough situation and ways to handle it.
2. Discuss examples in literature, history, or current events of the ways people handle tough situations.

Self Acceptance

Lesson 66: Handling the Ups and Downs

1. Why are things rough for me right now?

2. What are three things I can do?

3. Pick one and try it.

4. Pick another, if necessary, and try it.

SELF-ACCEPTANCE

Dennis Hanken, Ed.S. and Judith Kennedy, Ed.S.

Lesson 67: Be Yourself—Acceptance By Others

Objective: Students will identify reasons to be authentic, despite pressure to conform.

Materials Needed: Journals and clay.

Establish the Need: Make a design with the clay. Then, while talking about the pressures people, especially teenagers, have to conform to group standards and mores, mold and press the clay until it no longer resembles the first design. Discuss how people are like that clay. We start out with our own destinies, then the experiences and the people with whom we share our lives shape and mold us. Sometimes we are shaped to the point we are no longer recognizable.

Procedures:

Step 1: Model the skill:

Model using "Think Aloud" strategies—identifying reasons to be authentic.

1. What is being asked of me?
2. Is this something I want to do?
3. Make a choice based on my higher good.

Step 2: Role play with feedback:

A. Have your students journal what is important to them— what sets them apart from others.

B. Have them journal times they have made choices not in keeping with their authenticity.

Helpful Hints: The work on being oneself might bring up issues of sexual orientation. It might be good to have a counselor assist with this lesson.

Step 3: Transfer training

A. **School:** Ask the school counselor to come in and do a brief personality inventory with your students. The point will be to see how they are alike and different from each other.

B. **Home/Community:** Have your students ask a family member what personality characteristic they attribute to that student.

C. **Peers:** In small groups, have your students discuss the risks and pressures of being themselves.

Comments: The psychological work of teenagers is to find/create their own identity. This journey has many pitfalls. While trying to break out of the mode of our family, the temptation is great to swing too far into accepting our peers' ideas of who we are. Help your students see the benefits and risks of being truly themselves.

Extended Activities:

1. Arrange for speakers from the community who have dared to break out of the mode and be themselves.

2. Have your students make a design, picture, or some form of art that depicts who each is and put the designs together as a collage.

Self Acceptance

Lesson 67: Be Yourself—
Acceptance by Others

1. What is being asked of me?

2. Is this something I want to do?

3. Make a choice based on my higher good.

SELF-ACCEPTANCE

Lesson 68: Accentuate Your Strong Points

Objective: Students will identify strengths and weaknesses and make a plan for presenting their strengths.

Materials Needed: Journals.

Establish the Need: Read and discuss the following:

Michael Jordan is quoted as saying that he missed 3,000 free throws and only made 400. Perhaps he was not the world's greatest basketball player because he wasn't perfect. What did make him so great? How does he differ from Dennis Rodman? Albert Einstein was believed to be too stupid to be able to succeed in school, so his mother took him out and home schooled him.

1. How did each of these people accentuate their positive attributes?

2. Name some weaknesses of each.

3. Discuss other examples of success despite weaknesses.

Procedures:

Step 1:   Model the skill:

Model using "Think Aloud" strategies—identifying your strengths.

1. What do I do well?

2. How can I use that to succeed?

Step 2:   Role play with feedback:

Have your students journal listing every strength they can identify about themselves and how they might use those strengths toward a goal.

Step 3:   Transfer training

A. **School:** Lead a class discussion on the strengths needed to be successful at school, in sports, and in life.

B. **Home/Community:** Ask your students to journal what qualities are needed to have successful family relationships.

C. **Peers:** In small groups, have them brainstorm and list qualities needed to be a friend.

Comments: Students may need help identifying their strengths.

Extended Activities:

1. Have your students write a futuristic short story describing one of their strengths and how they have applied it to life.

2. Research a famous person of choice and determine how that person used his or her strengths to be successful.

Self Acceptance

Lesson 68: Accentuate Your Strong Points

1. What do I do well?

2. How can I use that to succeed?

SELF-ACCEPTANCE

Dennis Hanken, Ed.S. and Judith Kennedy, Ed.S.

Bibliography

Periodical

Rutherford, R.B. (July, 1997), "Why doesn't social skills training work?" *Council for Exceptional Children, 14.*

Books

Aesop. (1993). *Aesop's fables.* New York: Grosset & Dunlap.

Bodine, R., & Crawford, D., (1999). *Developing emotional intelligence.* Champaign, IL: Research Press.

Brockman, M.P. (1985). "Best practices in assessment of social skills and peer interaction" in *Best practices in school psychology.* Kent, OH: National Association of School Psychologists, 43-609.

Carlson, G.A., & Cantwell, D.P., (1982). *Journal of the American Academy of Child Psychology,* 21, 361-368.

Cartledge, G., & Fellows Milburn, J. (1986). *Teaching social skills to children.* Needham Heights, MA: Allyn & Bacon.

Frank, R.A., & Edwards, P.P. (1993). *Building self-esteem.* Portland, OR: Ednick Communications.

Gresham, F.M. (1992). "Best practice in social skills training" in *Best practices in school psychology.* Kent, OH: National Association of School Psychologists, 181-192.

Huggins, P., Wood Manion, D., & Moen, L. (1993). *Teaching friendship skills: Intermediate version.* Longmont, CO: Sopris West.

Kubler-Ross, E. (1969). *On death and dying.* New York: MacMillan.

Madaras, L. (1993). My *feelings, my self.* New York: Newmarket.

McGinnis, E., & Goldstein, A.P. (1997). *Skillstreaming the adolescent.* Champaign, IL: Research Press.

Myers, P. & Nance, D. (1986). *The upset book.* Notre Dame, IN: Academic Publications.

Nelson, R., Dandeneau, C., & Schrader, M., (1998). *Working with adolescents: Building effective communication and choice-making skills.* Minneapolis, MN: Educational Media Corporation.

Paterson, Katherine, 1977. *Bridge over Tabithia.* New York: Crowell.

Rich, D. (1992). *Megaskills.* New York: Houghton Mifflin.

Stark, K. (1990). *Childhood depression.* New York: Guilford.

Vernon, A. (1989). *Thinking, feeling, and behaving.* Champaign, IL: Research Press.

Dennis Hanken, Ed.S. and Judith Kennedy, Ed.S.